An Unusual Devotional for Usual Days

Rodney Charles Dutton

R. C. Dutton Books

ISBN – 13: 978-0-9993330-7-5

ISBN – 10: 0-9993330-7-0

R. C. Dutton Books

Dedicated to Don and Elizabeth Castiglioni who showed me hospitality, allowed me to stay at their home, during which I came up with the idea for a book of questions

#1

Can you give an example of foolishness? Foolishness is a clown crying in the streets, "Let's twist balloons into horses, and ride them into the valley of nails as we listen to the popping sounds."

Wisdom cries aloud in the street, in the markets she raises her voice; If you turn at my reproof, behold, I will pour out my spirit to you; I will make my words known to you.

Proverbs 1:20, 23

#2

Do you enjoy playing King of the Mountain? When I play King of the Mountain, everyone fights to be on top, but I am content to be King of the Valley, dwelling in peace.

You will keep him in perfect peace whose mind is stayed on you, because he trusts in you. Trust in the LORD forever, for the LORD GOD is an everlasting rock.

Isaiah 26:3, 4

Cloud Crown

The King of the mountains

Adorns His creation

With a cloud crown

That we may see its beauty

And look up toward

His heavenly throne

#3

In a desert, people have mirages about water. At sea, people see mirages of land. Why don't they just swap places, so they won't need to have optical illusions?

Let them thank the LORD for his steadfast love, for his wondrous works to the children of man! He turns rivers into a desert, springs of water into thirsty ground. He turns a desert into pools of water, a parched land into springs of water.

Psalm 107:31, 33, 35

#4

What is a question you might hear at a human organ parts store?

"Do you have a four-valve heart for a 1964 Italian male?"

And I will give you a new heart, and a new spirit I will put within you. And I will remove the heart of stone from your flesh and give you a heart of flesh. And I will put my Spirit within you, and cause you to walk in my statutes and be careful to obey my rules.

Ezekiel 36:26- 27

#5

Do you know the Kenny Roger's napkin philosophy? You've got to know when to hold 'em, know when to fold 'em, and know when to walk away.

Then Simon Peter came, following him, and went into the tomb. He saw the linen cloths lying there, and the face cloth, which had been on Jesus' head, not lying with the linen cloths but folded up in a place by itself.

John 20:6, 7

#6

Have you seen signs on an entrance that say, *Please Keep Door Closed*? If we can never open that door, why have one there to begin with?

"And to the angel of the church in Philadelphia write: The words of the holy one, the true one, who has the key of David, who opens and no one will shut, who shuts and no one opens."

Revelation 3:7

#7

Should we take ourselves seriously? No, we should learn to laugh at our mistakes. I have. Now you know why I laugh every day, all day long.

When the LORD restored the fortunes of Zion, we were like those who dream. Then our mouth was filled with laughter, and our tongue with shouts of joy; then they said among the nations, "The Lord has done great things for them."

Psalm 126:1- 2

#8

When I sneeze people say, "God bless you." Why don't people want me to be blessed when I burp or fart?

The Lord bless you and keep you; the Lord make his face to shine upon you and be gracious to you; the Lord lift up his countenance upon you and give you peace.

Numbers 6:24 -26

#9

What is a fall guy?

fall guy: n. a person who takes the blame for autumn leaves not being raked

"Blessed is the man who trusts in the Lord, whose trust is the Lord. He is like a tree planted by water, that sends out its roots by the stream, and does not fear when heat comes, for its leaves remain green, and is not anxious in the year of drought, for it does not cease to bear fruit."

Jeremiah 17:7- 8

#10

Have you ever seen a dog that was a scaredy-cat?

The wolf shall dwell with the lamb, and the leopard shall lie down with the young goat, and the calf and the lion and the fattened calf together; and a little child shall lead them. They shall not hurt or destroy in all my holy mountain; for the earth shall be full of the knowledge of the Lord as the waters cover the sea.

Isaiah 11:6, 9

#11

Is it just a coincidence that all peeping Tom's have the same name?

For the eyes of the Lord are on the righteous, and his ears are open to their prayer. But the face of the Lord is against those who do evil.

1 Peter 3:12

#12

If money grew on trees, do you think more people would become arborists?

Keep your life free from love of money, and be content with what you have, for he has said, "I will never leave you nor forsake you."

Hebrews 13:5

#13

Shouldn't we say, "It's all good or bad," instead of, "It's all good"? Bad things happen every day.

Do not be overcome by evil, but overcome evil with good.

Romans 12:21

#14

Did you know that lazy people are highly skilled at making their co-workers jobs more difficult?

Whoever is slack in his work is a brother to him who destroys.

Proverbs 18:9

#15

Is it correct to say, "I'm speaking off the cuff," when I'm wearing short sleeves?

Let your speech always be gracious, seasoned with salt, so that you may know how you ought to answer each person.

Colossians 4:6

#16

Why do shadows hide when there is complete darkness? I guess shadows are afraid of the dark.

For God gave us a spirit not of fear but of power and love and self-control.

2 Timothy 1:7

#17

Why was my teacher upset with me? She told me to read the whole paragraph to the class, and that's just what I did.

John ran very fast through the field of wild flowers shouting comma quotation mark I feel alive and full of joy exclamation point quotation mark The sun shined brightly on the golden blooming field comma while the birds circled overhead at midday period

Now Jesus did many other signs in the presence of the disciples, which are not written in this book; but these are written so that you may believe that Jesus is the Christ, the Son of God, and that by believing you may have life in his name.

John 20:30 - 31

#18

Shouldn't there be a seven-day weekend each week?

Slothfulness casts into a deep sleep, and an idle person will suffer hunger.

Proverbs 19:15

Onomatopoeia

The dove on the window sill
And the baby in the cradle cooed
The fly and the busy woman
Both buzzed about the house
The woman's husband and the dog
Barked continuously at her
The cow outside the window mooed
And the baby in the cradle pooed
Diaper duty
Just what the busy woman needed
Her husband doesn't give a crap
About his over-worked wife

#19

What is your favorite apple? My favorite is pineapple.

Keep me as the apple of your eye; hide me in the shadow of your wings, from the wicked who do me violence, my deadly enemies who surround me.

Psalm 17:8- 9

#20

If Earth was one big ocean, don't you think learning to swim should be made mandatory? Probably some people would disagree, saying, "We should not force people to learn to swim, individuals should be allowed to pursue and practice their natural right to sink."

Here is the sea, great and wide, which teems with creatures innumerable, living things both small and great.

Psalm 104:25

#21

Don't you think monsters should find a new place to hide? All children know they are hiding under the bed.

And they heard the sound of the Lord God walking in the garden in the cool of the day, and the man and his wife hid themselves from the presence of the Lord God among the trees of the garden.

Genesis 3:8

#22

What is your favorite action film this fall? I like Brown Leaf Down. It's about a fallen autumn leaf, and the race to rescue it before it's mulched by an enemy mower.

We have all become like one who is unclean, and all our righteous deeds are like a polluted garment. We all fade like a leaf, and our iniquities, like the wind, take us away.

Isaiah 64:6

#23

Did you know that people who suffer from night blindness are healed of this problem during the daytime?

As he passed by, he saw a man blind from birth. And his disciples asked him, "Rabbi, who sinned, this man or his parents, that he was born blind?" Jesus answered, "It was not that this man sinned, or his parents, but that the works of God might be displayed in him."

John 9:1- 3

#24

Why are there so many orphan highways? I keep seeing signs asking people to adopt them. Anyone want to be highway parents?

For all who are led by the Spirit of God are sons of God. For you did not receive the spirit of slavery to fall back into fear, but you have received the Spirit of adoption as sons, by whom we cry, "Abba! Father!"

Romans 8:14- 15

#25

Did you know that while humans sleep, cockroaches perform nightly their off-Broadway performance of *Infested Kitchen*?

Be glad, O children of Zion, and rejoice in the Lord your God, for he has given the early rain for your vindication; he has poured down for you abundant rain, the early and the latter rain, as before. The threshing floors shall be full of grain; the vats shall overflow with wine and oil.
I will restore to you the years that the swarming locust has eaten, the hopper, the destroyer, and the cutter, my great army, which I sent among you.

Joel 2:23- 25

#26

Has anyone ever told you they were on a quest to find themselves? My advice to them is, look in the mirror.

Whoever finds his life will lose it, and whoever loses his life for my sake will find it.

Matthew 10:39

#27

Did you know that people come in different flavors? Some are sweet, others are sour, a few are salty, and then, there are those who are an acquired taste. You must grow to love them over a long period of time.

For it is not an enemy who taunts me— then I could bear it; it is not an adversary who deals insolently with me— then I could hide from him. But it is you, a man, my equal, my companion, my familiar friend. We used to take sweet counsel together; within God's house we walked in the throng.

Psalm 55:12- 14

#28

Do you find trouble extremely troublesome? The trouble with trouble is that it comes at the most inconvenient times.

And we know that for those who love God all things work together for good, for those who are called according to his purpose.

Romans 8:28

#29

Are you an expert on romance? Even though the word *man* is found in *romance*, it doesn't mean men are experts in this subject.

Husbands, love your wives, as Christ loved the church and gave himself up for her, that he might sanctify her, having cleansed her by the washing of water with the word, so that he might present the church to himself in splendor, without spot or wrinkle or any such thing, that she might be holy and without blemish.

Ephesians 5:25- 27

#30

Is it true that when difficulties happen outside of us, they reveal what is inside us?

Count it all joy, my brothers, when you meet trials of various kinds, for you know that the testing of your faith produces steadfastness.

James 1:2- 3

#31

Have you ever been confused as to what something meant in a message you received? I wondered for a long time why my girlfriend was writing the word *ox* at the end of her letters. I was too shy to ask her what it meant, since she'd been writing that for more than a year. When I found out, I felt as dumb as an ox.

Where there are no oxen, the manger is clean, but abundant crops come by the strength of the ox.

Proverbs 14:4

#32

If some people are so good at trouble-shooting, why can't they shoot and kill trouble once and for all?

Jesus answered them, "Do you now believe? Behold, the hour is coming, indeed it has come, when you will be scattered, each to his own home, and will leave me alone. Yet I am not alone, for the Father is with me. I have said these things to you, that in me you may have peace. In the world you will have tribulation. But take heart; I have overcome the world."

John 16:31- 33

#33

Did you know that I never say the word *bad*? I was told not to use bad words.

No human being can tame the tongue. It is a restless evil, full of deadly poison. With it we bless our Lord and Father, and with it we curse people who are made in the likeness of God. From the same mouth come blessing and cursing. My brothers, these things ought not to be so.

James 3:8- 10

#34

What is a shoe maker's favorite dessert? Cobbler.

John the baptizer said, "I baptize you with water for repentance, but he who is coming after me is mightier than I, whose sandals I am not worthy to carry. He will baptize you with the Holy Spirit and fire."

Matthew 3:11

#35

Is it always an honor to be in the spotlight? Being in the spotlight is great for a performer, but it's the end of the drama for an escaped prisoner.

For at one time you were darkness, but now you are light in the Lord. Walk as children of light (for the fruit of light is found in all that is good and right and true).

Ephesians 5:8 – 9

#36

Why is pink the color of all elephants seen during hallucinations? I guess an uncommon hallucination would be a person seeing a white elephant. It seems that white elephants are very rare in the real world, and in delusional ones.

"Come now, let us reason together, says the Lord: though your sins are like scarlet, they shall be as white as snow; though they are red like crimson, they shall become like wool."

Isaiah 1:18

#37

Doesn't life sometimes feel like you're playing dodgeball with bowling balls?

For it has been granted to you that for the sake of Christ you should not only believe in him but also suffer for his sake.

Philippians 1:29

#38

Why doesn't sleeping on a memory foam pillow help us to remember? In the morning, I still forgot everything I dreamed during the night.

"If you were of the world, the world would love you as its own; but because you are not of the world, but I chose you out of the world, therefore the world hates you. Remember the word that I said to you: 'A servant is not greater than his master.' If they persecuted me, they will also persecute you. If they kept my word, they will also keep yours."

John 15:19- 20

One Last Stroke

He spilled his ink

They spilled his blood

The two mingled together

Becoming his greatest writing of all—Martyrdom.

#39

Do you know the name of the amnesiac guy's ex? Her name is *X*.

They said to him, "Why then did Moses command one to give a certificate of divorce and to send her away?" He said to them, "Because of your hardness of heart Moses allowed you to divorce your wives, but from the beginning it was not so. And I say to you: whoever divorces his wife, except for sexual immorality, and marries another, commits adultery."

Matthew 19:7-9

#40

Have you ever heard the phrase, "That's easier said than done"? I wish that was true concerning my past mistakes, because I made them easily.

The law of the Lord is perfect, reviving the soul; the testimony of the Lord is sure, making wise the simple; the precepts of the Lord are right, rejoicing the heart; the commandment of the Lord is pure, enlightening the eyes.

Psalm 19:7-8

#41

Some people strive to live in peace, united with others like the tightly twisted cords of a rope, but in the end, they are unsuccessful. They have transposed the *i* and *t* of *united*. Do you get *it*?

I appeal to you, brothers, by the name of our Lord Jesus Christ, that all of you agree, and that there be no divisions among you, but that you be united in the same mind and the same judgment.

1 Corinthians 1:10

#42

What is the definition of work?
work: v. a four-letter word that enables you to eat, so you have plenty of strength to complain about having to work

Whatever you do, work heartily, as for the Lord and not for men, knowing that from the Lord you will receive the inheritance as your reward. You are serving the Lord Christ.

Colossians 3:23- 24

#43

We should reverse things and work for two to four weeks a year, spending the rest of the time on vacation. Isn't that a good idea? That way we would look forward to our job, and say with excitement, "I'm going on work next week!"

Commit your work to the Lord, and your plans will be established.

Proverbs 16:3

#44

Did you know that lazy employees are often very good actors? Sometimes, they can make you think they are actually doing work.

The desire of the sluggard kills him, for his hands refuse to labor.

Proverbs 21:25

#45

Why does a nomad wander from place to place? It's not because they're mad at anybody at the last location. No, mad. Yes, adventure.

With my whole heart I seek you; let me not wander from your commandments!

Psalm 119:10

#46

Why do some people make resolutions they won't be able to keep every New Year? I guess it's their tradition.

"If you love me, you will keep my commandments."

John 14:15

#47

Have you ever heard your stomach speak? It can, but most of the time it only says, "I'm hungry!"

"Blessed are those who hunger and thirst for righteousness, for they shall be satisfied."

Matthew 5:6

#48

Have you ever seen people applaud when they are outside in the midst of mosquitos? Okay, maybe they're just trying to smash the mosquitos between their hands. We should give them a round of applause for that.

Clap your hands, all peoples! Shout to God with loud songs of joy!

Psalm 47:1

#49

If boxing rings were not square like a box, then what would boxers be called? Maybe triangulars, circlers, or trapezoidians.

I do not box as one beating the air. But I discipline my body and keep it under control, lest after preaching to others I myself should be disqualified.

1 Corinthians 9:26b- 27

#50

Do you know why pirates put X's on their maps? Pirates love buried treasure, so they put an *X* on the map to mark the spot where it's buried. The *X* represents a big hug.

For where your treasure is, there your heart will be also.

Matthew 6:21

#51

Do you know the meaning of *deadbeat*? A deadbeat is a drummer who is too lazy to go to work and beat his drum, preferring to beat his chest and say, "Woe is me."

The sluggard says, "There is a lion in the road! There is a lion in the streets!"

Proverbs 26:13

#52

Did you know that insects were born with more than one antenna long before the invention of the radio? What music did bugs listen to before radio stations existed?

Go to the ant, O sluggard; consider her ways, and be wise.

Proverbs 6:6

#53

Can you make the silent k sound in knife? You can do it! Just take a stab at it.

"Teach me, and I will be silent; make me understand how I have gone astray."

Job 6:24

#54

What should we call a person who is substituting for a substitute violin teacher? Third string?

Praise him with tambourine and dance; praise him with strings and pipe!

Psalm 150:4

#55

Did you know that every workday is like a holiday for people who love their jobs?

Rejoice always, pray without ceasing, give thanks in all circumstances; for this is the will of God in Christ Jesus for you.

1 Thessalonians 5:16- 18

#56

If every office worker wore blinders, would there still be a need for cubicles?

Therefore, since we are surrounded by so great a cloud of witnesses, let us also lay aside every weight, and sin which clings so closely, and let us run with endurance the race that is set before us, looking to Jesus, the founder and perfecter of our faith.

Hebrews 12:1- 2b

#57

Did you know that foodies love hanging out with their buds to eat? Their taste buds, that is.

Oh, taste and see that the Lord is good! Blessed is the man who takes refuge in him!

Psalm 34:8

#58

Do you enjoy peppery, hot food? I like spicy food, but I don't like it so hot that the only thing I taste is pain.

How sweet are your words to my taste, sweeter than honey to my mouth!

Psalm 119:103

#59

What could be more ideal for a couch potato than a sofa that turns into a bed?

As a door turns on its hinges, so does a sluggard on his bed.

Proverbs 26:14

#60

Do you think animals at the zoo ever say, "This place is a real zoo!" when they complain about their crazy surroundings?

Peter went up on the housetop about the sixth hour to pray. And he became hungry and wanted something to eat, but while they were preparing it, he fell into a trance and saw the heavens opened and something like a great sheet descending, being let down by its four corners upon the earth. In it were all kinds of animals and reptiles and birds of the air. And there came a voice to him: "Rise, Peter; kill and eat." But Peter said, "By no means, Lord; for I have never eaten anything that is common or unclean." And the voice came to him again a second time, "What God has made clean, do not call common." This happened three times, and the thing was taken up at once to heaven.

Acts 10:9b- 16

#61

Did you know that criminals who escape from prison are always big men? Yes, that's why they say they are *at large.*

About midnight Paul and Silas were praying and singing hymns to God, and the prisoners were listening to them, and suddenly there was a great earthquake, so that the foundations of the prison were shaken. And immediately all the doors were opened, and everyone's bonds were unfastened. When the jailer woke and saw that the prison doors were open, he drew his sword and was about to kill himself, supposing that the prisoners had escaped. But Paul cried with a loud voice, "Do not harm yourself, for we are all here."

Acts 16:25- 28

#62

Is it always good to strive to be at the top? No, sometimes it's not good, like being on the F.B.I.'s top-ten most wanted list.

And they had then a notorious prisoner called Barabbas. So when they had gathered, Pilate said to them, "Whom do you want me to release for you: Barabbas, or Jesus who is called Christ?" For he knew that it was out of envy that they had delivered him up. Besides, while he was sitting on the judgment seat, his wife sent word to him, "Have nothing to do with that righteous man, for I have suffered much because of him today in a dream." Now the chief priests and the elders persuaded the crowd to ask for Barabbas and destroy Jesus.

Matthew 27:16- 20

Creative Words

In the beginning nothing was there,
Only the Creator, the Bible does declare.
His Creative words brought forth and caused to be
Wondrous things like a giraffe and the sycamore tree.
His words brought forth buzzing from the wings of
the bee,
Also chirping and singing from the first birds with
glee.
He brought forth new creatures arrayed in vibrant
colors
Cheetahs, peacocks, and tigers along with many
others.
These things were created and did not exist eternally,
God released His plans through words and they
became reality.
A multitude of life did appear at His decree,
From the mouth of the One whom in persons is three.
God formed man from the dust to bear his likeness,
To love one another with goodness and kindness.
God is great and the Creator of all,
He is LORD of everyone both big and small.
Hallelujah to our Maker, our great God and King,
He is worthy of praise, so lift your voice and sing.

#63

Can my shirt be called a *muscle shirt* even if my arms are like toothpicks?

But God chose what is foolish in the world to shame the wise; God chose what is weak in the world to shame the strong;

1 Corinthians 1:27

#64

What is one difference between a prison and a zoo? Prisons have a lot more inmates who are primates.

Remember those who are in prison, as though in prison with them, and those who are mistreated, since you also are in the body.

Hebrews 13:3

#65

Can you spell *good* without God? O, I see.

Praise the Lord! Oh give thanks to the Lord, for he is good, for his steadfast love endures forever!

Psalm 106:1

#66

Shouldn't laying hens have squatter's rights?

"If you come across a bird's nest in any tree or on the ground, with young ones or eggs and the mother sitting on the young or on the eggs, you shall not take the mother with the young."

Deuteronomy 22:6

#67

Did you know that a *fan club* is not a club used to beat unruly fans?

Whoever spares the rod hates his son, but he who loves him is diligent to discipline him.

Proverbs 13:24

#68

Why does the wind only blow on windy days?

"The wind blows where it wishes, and you hear its sound, but you do not know where it comes from or where it goes. So it is with everyone who is born of the Spirit."

John 3:8

#69

Could a mosquito be referred to as a flying phlebotomist since it draws blood?

For the life of the flesh is in the blood, and I have given it for you on the altar to make atonement for your souls, for it is the blood that makes atonement by the life.

Leviticus 17:11

#70

Is *field of tears* another way to say *onion patch*?

"We remember the fish we ate in Egypt that cost nothing, the cucumbers, the melons, the leeks, the onions, and the garlic. But now our strength is dried up, and there is nothing at all but this manna to look at."

Numbers 11:5- 6

#71

What do bottled time, and bottled wine have in common? They both age.

I have been young, and now am old, yet I have not seen the righteous forsaken or his children begging for bread.

Psalm 37:25

#72

X marks the spot. Do we really need to mark the spot or stain? Aren't they already visible enough?

Though you wash yourself with lye and use much soap, the stain of your guilt is still before me, declares the Lord God.

Jeremiah 2:22

#73

People often associate being crazy with bananas. Why don't we also use other fruit to describe insane behavior? Maybe, "They're completely grapes," or, "Those people have gone mangos."

"Beware of false prophets, who come to you in sheep's clothing but inwardly are ravenous wolves. You will recognize them by their fruits. Are grapes gathered from thorn bushes, or figs from thistles? So, every healthy tree bears good fruit, but the diseased tree bears bad fruit."

Matthew 7:15- 17

#74

When professional stunt people do dangerous tricks they say, "Don't try this at home." Do they want us to try these dangerous stunts at our workplaces?

In peace I will both lie down and sleep; for you alone, O Lord, make me dwell in safety.

Psalm 4:8

#75

A lot of mushrooms are potty trained. Haven't you heard of toadstools?

One of them went out into the field to gather herbs, and found a wild vine and gathered from it his lap full of wild gourds, and came and cut them up into the pot of stew, not knowing what they were. And they poured out some for the men to eat. But while they were eating of the stew, they cried out, "O man of God, there is death in the pot!" And they could not eat it. He said, "Then bring flour." And he threw it into the pot and said, "Pour some out for the men, that they may eat." And there was no harm in the pot.

2 Kings 4:39- 41

#76

What do most snakes and most people agree on? Both don't like each other on days that end with *y*.

Then the Lord God said to the woman, "What is this that you have done?"
The woman said, "The serpent deceived me, and I ate."
The Lord God said to the serpent, "Because you have done this, cursed are you above all livestock and above all beasts of the field; on your belly you shall go, and dust you shall eat all the days of your life. I will put enmity between you and the woman, and between your offspring and her offspring;
he shall bruise your head, and you shall bruise his heel."

Genesis 3:13- 15

#77

Why do people tell their friends who've just broken up that there are "plenty of fish in the sea"? Are they saying their previous relationship was a little fishy?

Do not be unequally yoked with unbelievers. For what partnership has righteousness with lawlessness? Or what fellowship has light with darkness? What accord has Christ with Belial? Or what portion does a believer share with an unbeliever?

2 Corinthians 6:14- 15

#78

Did you know that the F.B.I. has a lot of problems with its plumbing? Yes, they are always talking about government leaks.

A continual dripping on a rainy day and a quarrelsome wife are alike;

Proverbs 27:15

#79

What brings you joy? One thing that brings me joy is *joy*.

You make known to me the path of life; in your presence there is fullness of joy; at your right hand are pleasures forevermore.

Psalm 16:11

#80

Do you have any friends who live in a gated community? Living in a gated community is fine, but I prefer to live in a gated and fenced community. It's safer.

"Enter by the narrow gate. For the gate is wide and the way is easy that leads to destruction, and those who enter by it are many. For the gate is narrow and the way is hard that leads to life, and those who find it are few."

Matthew 7:13- 14

Revelation 3:20

Persistently you knock in love,
A soft song
Gently tapped on my door in perfect rhythm.
The chorus says, "I love you,
I love you,
Let me love you more."

Though you live inside me
I have closed the door to your fellowship.

You are here with me
But I am not fully here with you.
I do love you,
But, there are some locks
That need to be removed.

Many times, I cannot hear
The sound of your knock,
Or your voice calling out my name,
For the responsibilities of life
Are frequently louder,
Other times
I hear the sound
But, it's an annoyance
For I desire to do other things at that moment
But, when I slow down enough to hear my heartbeat
Your gentle knocking permeates me

With its comforting, melodious chords of love.

With my mind, heart, and soul
I crack the door open
As the radiant beams of light
Reach deep inside,
Caressing me in a warm embrace.

Without reserve I allow the door to swing fully open.
Jesus, your presence envelopes me like a letter
Sealed inside its paper vehicle.

The song has transitioned into a love letter.
Read to me,
As you and I dine without notice of the hours.
With my hungry heart we engage in conversation
Accompanied by my listening soul.

Let me write it on my doorposts,
I desire that the door of my heart
Would forever be open
For continual fellowship with you.

#81

A checkered past. Does that mean someone who was a former checkers champion?

And there came out from the camp of the Philistines a champion named Goliath of Gath, whose height was six cubits and a span. And the Philistine said, "I defy the ranks of Israel this day. Give me a man, that we may fight together." And David put his hand in his bag and took out a stone and slung it and struck the Philistine on his forehead. The stone sank into his forehead, and he fell on his face to the ground.

1 Samuel 17:4, 10, 49

#82

A *seaport* is on the sea. Why is an *airport* on the land?

But Jonah rose to flee to Tarshish from the presence of the Lord. He went down to Joppa and found a ship going to Tarshish. So he paid the fare and went down into it, to go with them to Tarshish, away from the presence of the Lord.

Jonah 1:3

#83

Many times, there is an X on a stage or film set, so performers know where they are supposed to stand. Why don't we have X's for politicians during their speeches, so they will know where they should stand on certain issues?

"Give justice to the weak and the fatherless; maintain the right of the afflicted and the destitute. Rescue the weak and the needy; deliver them from the hand of the wicked."

Psalm 82:3- 4

#84

Don't you feel sorry for irresponsible people? They never have enough time in a year to waste. Good thing they are given a little extra time on leap years.

Look carefully then how you walk, not as unwise but as wise, making the best use of the time, because the days are evil.

Ephesians 5:15- 16

#85

Is it true that for a lot of people a *Wet Paint, Please Don't Touch* sign is interpreted as *Wet Paint, Please Touch*? I guess the word *don't* is whitewashed in their mind.

If with Christ you died to the elemental spirits of the world, why, as if you were still alive in the world, do you submit to regulations— "Do not handle, Do not taste, Do not touch" (referring to things that all perish as they are used)—according to human precepts and teachings?

Colossians 2:20- 22

#86

Did you know that nocturnal animals were created to work the graveyard shift?

"We must work the works of him who sent me while it is day; night is coming, when no one can work. As long as I am in the world, I am the light of the world."

John 9:4- 5

#87

Did you know that every day is Monday for people who hate their jobs?

If anyone is not willing to work, let him not eat. For we hear that some among you walk in idleness, not busy at work, but busybodies. Now such persons we command and encourage in the Lord Jesus Christ to do their work quietly and to earn their own living.

2 Thessalonians 3:10b- 12

#88

Do you think windchimes are a better idea than earthquake chimes?

And Jesus cried out again with a loud voice and yielded up his spirit. And behold, the curtain of the temple was torn in two, from top to bottom. And the earth shook, and the rocks were split. The tombs also were opened. And many bodies of the saints who had fallen asleep were raised, and coming out of the tombs after his resurrection they went into the holy city and appeared to many.

Matthew 27:50- 53

Scheduled Quake

Shaking and rattling
With a loud sound
Inside my apartment
Three stories above ground

It's not an earthquake
Though the building did tremble
But an Elevated train
Just outside my window

Click Clack
Click Clack
Off my walls
Echoed back

The A-train
On its way
Brooklyn Bound
From Rockaway

A few seconds later
The roar left at last
Just wait a few minutes
The next train will go past

When renting a place
I should've given more thought
To the train tracks outside
Versus the cheap rent I got

#89

Is it wrong to call it a *life preserver* if the person wearing it is stranded in shark-infested waters?

For whoever would save his life will lose it, but whoever loses his life for my sake will find it.

Matthew 16:25

#90

Don't you think it would be better to be stranded on an island with desserts (a desserted island,) than on a regular deserted island?

But striking a reef, they ran the vessel aground. The bow stuck and remained immovable, and the stern was being broken up by the surf. The soldiers' plan was to kill the prisoners, lest any should swim away and escape. But the centurion, wishing to save Paul, kept them from carrying out their plan. He ordered those who could swim to jump overboard first and make for the land.

Acts 27:41- 43

#91

Why don't more people become make-up artists for on-air radio performers? This field is practically untouched.

Do not let your adorning be external—the braiding of hair and the putting on of gold jewelry, or the clothing you wear—but let your adorning be the hidden person of the heart with the imperishable beauty of a gentle and quiet spirit, which in God's sight is very precious.

1 Peter 3:3- 4

#92

Did you know that many individuals have trouble telling people *no*? I don't know why—both *yes* and *no* are one-syllable words. One should be just as easy to say as the other.

But above all, my brothers, do not swear, either by heaven or by earth or by any other oath, but let your "yes" be yes and your "no" be no, so that you may not fall under condemnation.

James 5:12

#93

Why don't individuals like to go to court? Because nobody likes to be around people who are always judging them.

When one of you has a grievance against another, does he dare go to law before the unrighteous instead of the saints? Or do you not know that the saints will judge the world? And if the world is to be judged by you, are you incompetent to try trivial cases? Do you not know that we are to judge angels? How much more, then, matters pertaining to this life!

1 Corinthians 6:1- 3

#94

Have you ever heard of an Apparel Lunar Eclipse? It's when someone's pants are pulled all the way up, so they can't moon you.

When he opened the sixth seal, I looked, and behold, there was a great earthquake, and the sun became black as sackcloth, the full moon became like blood.

Revelation 6:12

#95

Some people leave bread crumbs to find their way back in case they get lost. Shouldn't they keep the bread, so they will have something to eat if they do get lost?

So he told them this parable: "What man of you, having a hundred sheep, if he has lost one of them, does not leave the ninety-nine in the open country, and go after the one that is lost, until he finds it? And when he has found it, he lays it on his shoulders, rejoicing. Just so, I tell you, there will be more joy in heaven over one sinner who repents than over ninety-nine righteous persons who need no repentance."

Luke 15:3- 5, 7

#96

Have you ever noticed that inconvenience and improvement often happen at the same location?

For I consider that the sufferings of this present time are not worth comparing with the glory that is to be revealed to us.

Romans 8:18

#97

Why is making snow angels more popular than making sand angels? Making sand angels is good for exfoliating your skin.

And to which of the angels has he ever said, "Sit at my right hand until I make your enemies a footstool for your feet"? Are they not all ministering spirits sent out to serve for the sake of those who are to inherit salvation?

Hebrews 1:13- 14

#98

Have you heard erroneous reports that state Michael Jackson was the first person to moon-walk? Neil Armstrong was really the first. That was one small step for this man to correct that mistake.

I have taught you the way of wisdom; I have led you in the paths of uprightness. When you walk, your step will not be hampered, and if you run, you will not stumble. Keep hold of instruction; do not let go; guard her, for she is your life.

Proverbs 4:11- 13

#99

Are a blank stare and a blank check similar? I guess so, because you can fill in the blanks on both for yourself.

So we do not lose heart. Though our outer self is wasting away, our inner self is being renewed day by day. For this light momentary affliction is preparing for us an eternal weight of glory beyond all comparison, as we look not to the things that are seen but to the things that are unseen. For the things that are seen are transient, but the things that are unseen are eternal.

2 Corinthians 4:16- 18

#100

Why do we have cups we cannot drink from? Like hiccups.

He took a cup, and when he had given thanks he gave it to them, saying, "Drink of it, all of you, for this is my blood of the covenant, which is poured out for many for the forgiveness of sins."

Matthew 26:27- 28

#101

Do you think collecting rocks is a good hobby? I love to search for interesting rocks. I've thought about getting a dog to help me find rocks. I'm going to adopt a rock hound.

As he was drawing near—already on the way down the Mount of Olives—the whole multitude of his disciples began to rejoice and praise God with a loud voice for all the mighty works that they had seen, saying, "Blessed is the King who comes in the name of the Lord! Peace in heaven and glory in the highest!" And some of the Pharisees in the crowd said to him, "Teacher, rebuke your disciples." He answered, "I tell you, if these were silent, the very stones would cry out."

Luke 19:37- 40

#102

Why do so many people engage in shrub abuse?
Don't beat around the bush. State your point directly.

And the angel of the Lord appeared to him in a flame
of fire out of the midst of a bush. He looked, and
behold, the bush was burning, yet it was not
consumed. And Moses said, "I will turn aside to see
this great sight, why the bush is not burned." When
the Lord saw that he turned aside to see, God called
to him out of the bush, "Moses, Moses!" And he said,
"Here I am." Then he said, "Do not come near; take
your sandals off your feet, for the place on which you
are standing is holy ground."

Exodus 3:2- 5

#103

Why do some companies have very unusual
departments? I just received a duplicate message from
the office of redundancy. I guess it's business as
usual. I guess it's business as usual.

Rejoice in the Lord always; again I will say, rejoice.

Philippians 4:4

#104

Should apparel be called *clothing* if it's not made from cloth?

Now there is great gain in godliness with contentment, for we brought nothing into the world, and we cannot take anything out of the world. But if we have food and clothing, with these we will be content.

1 Timothy 6:6- 8

#105

If you're dieting, doesn't that mean you're seeking to be a loser? I guess it is good to be a loser sometimes.

"For it seemed good to the Holy Spirit and to us to lay no greater burden on you than these few requirements: You must abstain from eating food offered to idols, from consuming blood or the meat of strangled animals, and from sexual immorality. If you do this, you will do well. Farewell."

Acts 15:28- 29

#106

Why does a river run, while most ponds have standing water? Is it because pond water is lazy, and rivers are into fitness?

"Whoever believes in me, as the Scripture has said, 'Out of his heart will flow rivers of living water.'" Now this he said about the Spirit, whom those who believed in him were to receive, for as yet the Spirit had not been given, because Jesus was not yet glorified.

John 7:38- 39

#107

Why do we often use *up* for good or positive things, and *down* for bad or negative things? For instance, "My internet is down," or, "She's moving up in the company." Keep your chin up and don't let this directional dilemma get you down.

I lift up my eyes to the hills. From where does my help come? My help comes from the Lord, who made heaven and earth.

Psalm 121:1- 2

#108

Did you know that dogs and babies have different potty methods? Dogs look for a perfect place to poop. For babies, everywhere is a perfect poop place.

And at noon Elijah mocked them (the prophets of Baal), saying, "Cry aloud, for he is a god. Either he is musing, or he is relieving himself, or he is on a journey, or perhaps he is asleep and must be awakened."

1 Kings 18:27

#109

What is a definition of money?
money: n. currency that a lot of people use to buy things they don't need

And my God will supply every need of yours according to his riches in glory in Christ Jesus. To our God and Father be glory forever and ever. Amen.

Philippians 4:19- 20

Canine Conditions

The wind howls

Trees wag their branches

Dropped leaves learn to roll over

Fallen sticks wait to play fetch

Summer lovers say,

"This day has gone to the dogs."

#110

Some health professionals tell their patients, "Listen to your body." Why do they want us to focus on burp and fart sounds?

For just as the body is one and has many members, and all the members of the body, though many, are one body, so it is with Christ. For in one Spirit we were all baptized into one body—Jews or Greeks, slaves or free—and all were made to drink of one Spirit.

1 Corinthians 12:12, 13

#111

We often say, "Have a great weekend!" Why don't we say, "Have a great weekstart"? Don't we need more well-wishes at the start of the week than at the end?

Now when he (Jesus) rose early on the first day of the week, he appeared first to Mary Magdalene, from whom he had cast out seven demons.

Mark 16:9

#112

Road questions to turbo-charge your mind and drive your imagination into the fast lane:

Why do we have ramps on interstate highways that are not good for jumps?

Are cobblestone streets built for shoe makers to drive on?

Can you build a highway in a valley?

If someone practices driving in a cul-de-sac, does that mean their driving exam is in the bag?

That very day two of them were going to a village named Emmaus, about seven miles from Jerusalem, and they were talking with each other about all these things that had happened. While they were talking and discussing together, Jesus himself drew near and went with them. They said to each other, "Did not our hearts burn within us while he talked to us on the road, while he opened to us the Scriptures?"

Luke 24:13- 15, 32

#113

What is the defintion of a history museum?

history museum: n. a museum where you go to visit the past while your time travel machine is being repaired

Therefore do not be ashamed of the testimony about our Lord, nor of me his prisoner, but share in suffering for the gospel by the power of God, who saved us and called us to a holy calling, not because of our works but because of his own purpose and grace, which he gave us in Christ Jesus before the ages began.

2 Timothy 1:8- 9

#114

Do you know what force field means?

force field: n. a field where Jedi's meet to practice using the force

All flesh is grass, and all its beauty is like the flower of the field. The grass withers, the flower fades, but the word of our God will stand forever.

Isaiah 40:6b, 8

#115

Is it important for us to be driven in our work? If I had more drive, I would become a chauffeur.

The Egyptians pursued and went in after them into the midst of the sea, all Pharaoh's horses, his chariots, and his horsemen. And in the morning watch the Lord in the pillar of fire and of cloud looked down on the Egyptian forces and threw the Egyptian forces into a panic, clogging their chariot wheels so that they drove heavily. And the Egyptians said, "Let us flee from before Israel, for the Lord fights for them against the Egyptians."

Exodus 14:23- 25

#116

When people say that they love me, are they telling me that because Jesus said, "Love your enemies"?

Love your enemies and pray for those who persecute you, so that you may be sons of your Father who is in heaven. For he makes his sun rise on the evil and on the good, and sends rain on the just and on the unjust.

Matthew 5:44b- 45

#117

Why aren't our bosses clearer in their instructions? My boss told me, "I want you to take your work to the next level." Then, a few days later he says, "When I said you need to take your work to the next level, I meant up, not down."

Now he tells me.

Commit your work to the Lord, and your plans will be established.

Proverbs 16:3

#118

Did you know that a time capsule is not a medication you take to help you remember the past?

"Remember not the former things, nor consider the things of old. Behold, I am doing a new thing; now it springs forth, do you not perceive it? I will make a way in the wilderness and rivers in the desert."

Isaiah 43:18-19

#119

Did you know that concrete workers have a lot of concrete thoughts?

And they said to one another, "Come, let us make bricks, and burn them thoroughly." And they had brick for stone, and bitumen for mortar. Then they said, "Come, let us build ourselves a city and a tower with its top in the heavens, and let us make a name for ourselves, lest we be dispersed over the face of the whole earth."

Genesis 11:3-4

#120

Did you know that some foods can speak? Yes, but only after you eat them.

And the tempter came and said to him, "If you are the Son of God, command these stones to become loaves of bread." But he answered, "It is written, 'Man shall not live by bread alone, but by every word that comes from the mouth of God.'"

Matthew 4:3- 4

#121

Sometimes when you ask people how they are doing, they say, "About average." Are they talking about the national average, or the international average?

Beloved, I pray that all may go well with you and that you may be in good health, as it goes well with your soul.

3 John 2

#122

Does *suspended animation* mean to stop working on an animated movie because of health problems?

Is anyone among you sick? Let him call for the elders of the church, and let them pray over him, anointing him with oil in the name of the Lord. And the prayer of faith will save the one who is sick, and the Lord will raise him up. And if he has committed sins, he will be forgiven.

James 5:14- 15

#123

Why don't many children want to be farmers when they grow up? Because a lot of kids don't like to eat vegetables, much less grow them.

Be patient, therefore, brothers, until the coming of the Lord. See how the farmer waits for the precious fruit of the earth, being patient about it, until it receives the early and the late rains. You also, be patient. Establish your hearts, for the coming of the Lord is at hand.

James 5:7- 8

#124

Did you know that no one has ever been stranded on a deserted island? As soon as they get there, it's no longer deserted.

I, John, your brother and partner in the tribulation and the kingdom and the patient endurance that are in Jesus, was on the island called Patmos on account of the word of God and the testimony of Jesus.

Revelation 1:9

#125

Why do people go window shopping at clothing stores? Shouldn't they go window shopping at window stores?

But if God so clothes the grass, which is alive in the field today, and tomorrow is thrown into the oven, how much more will he clothe you, O you of little faith!

Luke 12:28

#126

Do you have a bucket list? The first thing on my bucket list is to buy a bucket. The second thing is to return the bucket and get my money back before I kick the bucket.

Behold, the Lord God comes with might, and his arm rules for him; behold, his reward is with him, and his recompense before him. Behold, the nations are like a drop from a bucket, and are accounted as the dust on the scales; behold, he takes up the coastlands like fine dust.

Isaiah 40:10,15

#127

If you scratch the back of your imagination, will the itch grow stronger?

Being then God's offspring, we ought not to think that the divine being is like gold or silver or stone, an image formed by the art and imagination of man.

Acts 17:29

#128

Is it okay to drink spring water in the winter?

Jesus said to her, "Everyone who drinks of this water will be thirsty again, but whoever drinks of the water that I will give him will never be thirsty again. The water that I will give him will become in him a spring of water welling up to eternal life."

John 4:13- 14

#129

Do you know what a clown says when he announces his retirement? "I'm going to stop clowning around and take life seriously."

The way of a fool is right in his own eyes, but a wise man listens to advice.

Proverbs 12:15

#130

Did you know that a *headstone* is not a primitive pillow?

So early in the morning Jacob took the stone that he had put under his head and set it up for a pillar and poured oil on the top of it.

Genesis 28:18

#131

The teacher asked the student, "What is knowledge?" The student hesitated for a few seconds before he replied, "I know I should know this."

The fear of the Lord is the beginning of knowledge; fools despise wisdom and instruction.

Proverbs 1:7

#132

What is a weed root? A weed root is the root of all lawn evil.

For the love of money is a root of all kinds of evils. It is through this craving that some have wandered away from the faith and pierced themselves with many pangs.

1 Timothy 6:10

#133

Do you like apple-fritters? Apple-fritters are one of my favorite baked goods. I'm not sure where they find all the fresh fritters to make them. Probably on a fritter farm.

A word fitly spoken is like apples of gold in a setting of silver.

Proverbs 25:11

#134

Did you know that the *fountain of youth* does not refer to the stream of urine that might jet out at you when you are changing a baby's diaper?

The fear of the Lord is a fountain of life, that one may turn away from the snares of death.

Proverbs 14:27

#135

Have you seen cookware in stores from the new company Angry Chef? They sell durable pots and pans for cooks who are always flying off the handle.

Be angry and do not sin; do not let the sun go down on your anger, and give no opportunity to the devil.

Ephesians 4:26- 27

#136

Is it okay to use a night-light next to a day bed?

Yours is the day, yours also the night; you have established the heavenly lights and the sun.

Psalm 74:16

#137

Do you know the twelve steps to a good cup of coffee? It's the distance from my bedroom to my kitchen.

The steps of a man are established by the Lord, when he delights in his way;

Psalm 37:2

#138

If cabbage was our country's currency, I would try to produce a cash crop. Can you wrap your head around my cabbage idea?

Honor the Lord with your wealth and with the first fruits of all your produce;

Proverbs 3:9

Ground Coffee

Snow is falling

I am rising

From the icy ground

No one is around

To laugh at me

Or help me up

I think I broke

My coffee cup

But it was good

To the last drop

#139

Erasers on the end of pencils are proof that we make mistakes. Does that mean that people who use ink pens think they're perfect?

For all have sinned and fall short of the glory of God.

Romans 3:23

#140

Did you know dogs are very environmental and like to recycle? That's why they eat their own vomit.

Like a dog that returns to his vomit is a fool who repeats his folly.

Proverbs 26:11

#141

Did you know that some people don't deal well with change in their lives? Yes, they prefer to use paper money.

Jesus Christ is the same yesterday and today and forever.

Hebrews 13:8

#142

Since a cheerful heart is good medicine, does that make comedians health care professionals?

A joyful heart is good medicine, but a crushed spirit dries up the bones.

Proverbs 17:22

#143

Why don't we have leash laws for cats? I think it's because the authorities know that cats don't like to be seen in public with their owners.

The wicked flee when no one pursues, but the righteous are bold as a lion.

Proverbs 28:1

#144

Do pilots experience joy flying because planes have joy sticks?

You have put more joy in my heart than they have when their grain and wine abound.

Psalm 4:7

#145

Did you know that the exterior is where your ex lives?

"Woe to you, scribes and Pharisees, hypocrites! For you clean the outside of the cup and the plate, but inside they are full of greed and self-indulgence."

Matthew 23:25

#146

Do you know the name of Cinderella's perfume-loving sister? Her name was Citronella.

Oil and perfume make the heart glad, and the sweetness of a friend comes from his earnest counsel.

Proverbs 27:9

#147

We call them *parking lots*, but it's usually difficult to find a place to park. Don't you think we should call them *parking less* instead?

"He must increase, but I must decrease."

John 3:30

#148

When I buy a bottle of artificial tears, were they harvested from people who shed insincere tears during sad moments?

You have kept count of my tossings; put my tears in your bottle. Are they not in your book?

Psalm 56:8

#149

I've heard some people say, "If a black cat crosses your path, you will have bad luck." If a white cat crosses your path, will you have good luck?

And the Lord restored the fortunes of Job, when he had prayed for his friends. And the Lord gave Job twice as much as he had before. Then came to him all his brothers and sisters and all who had known him before, and ate bread with him in his house. And they showed him sympathy and comforted him for all the evil that the Lord had brought upon him. And each of them gave him a piece of money and a ring of gold.

Job 42:10- 11

Raining Tears

Your tears of concern

Gently water the weak and sickly ones

That struggle to survive

In the shadows of the un-nurtured soil

#150

Has the following been your experience? Shoes have tongues but don't speak, and a lot of them have bad breath.

Look at the ships also: though they are so large and are driven by strong winds, they are guided by a very small rudder wherever the will of the pilot directs. So also the tongue is a small member, yet it boasts of great things. How great a forest is set ablaze by such a small fire!

James 3:4- 5

#151

Why is *big* such a small word?

Bless the Lord, O my soul! O Lord my God, you are very great! You are clothed with splendor and majesty, covering yourself with light as with a garment, stretching out the heavens like a tent.

Psalm 104:1- 2

#152

Why do they have book signings? Books can't write their names.

King Belshazzar made a great feast for a thousand of his lords and drank wine in front of the thousand. Then they brought in the golden vessels that had been taken out of the temple, the house of God in Jerusalem, and the king and his lords, his wives, and his concubines drank from them. They drank wine and praised the gods of gold and silver, bronze, iron, wood, and stone.

Immediately the fingers of a human hand appeared and wrote on the plaster of the wall of the king's palace, opposite the lampstand. And the king saw the hand as it wrote. Then the king's color changed, and his thoughts alarmed him; his limbs gave way, and his knees knocked together.

Daniel 5:1, 3- 6

#153

What is a licensed carpenter? A person who can legally drive a Class A nail.

And on the Sabbath he began to teach in the synagogue, and many who heard him were astonished, saying, "Where did this man get these things? What is the wisdom given to him? How are such mighty works done by his hands? Is not this the carpenter, the son of Mary and brother of James and Joses and Judas and Simon? And are not his sisters here with us?" And they took offense at him.

Mark 6:2- 3

#154

How do you feel when people judge your writings and point out all your mistakes? A sloppy writer writes wrongs, and an efficient editor rights wrongs.

All Scripture is breathed out by God and profitable for teaching, for reproof, for correction, and for training in righteousness.

2 Timothy 3:16

Supportive

Watching from the shadows

Standing in the background

Cheering from behind

She supported from a distance

#155

Did you hear about the book that was picked up by the police? He was booked on suspicion of being a bookie. The judge listened to the book's story, and then, threw the book at him saying, "It seems that you are promoting a plot." Later, the book was released because the prosecution didn't do things by the book.

Now there are also many other things that Jesus did. Were every one of them to be written, I suppose that the world itself could not contain the books that would be written.

John 21:25

#156

Have you ever heard people say this? "Don't judge a person until you have walked in their shoes." If that's the case, I will never judge anyone. I don't want to get athlete's foot from wearing other people's shoes.

My son, if sinners entice you, do not consent. My son, do not walk in the way with them; hold back your foot from their paths.

Proverbs 1:10, 15

#157

You have probably heard the saying, "There's an elephant in the room." Where do all these elephants come from? How do they know when there's a big issue everyone is aware of, but are choosing to ignore, because it's uncomfortable to discuss? Is there an elephant warning system that alerts them of this situation?

Whoever speaks the truth gives honest evidence, but a false witness utters deceit.

Proverbs 12:17

#158

People build bird houses and dog houses. Why are we willing for the other animals to be homeless?

And a scribe came up and said to him, "Teacher, I will follow you wherever you go." And Jesus said to him, "Foxes have holes, and birds of the air have nests, but the Son of Man has nowhere to lay his head."

Matthew 8:19- 20

#159

What do a daily routine and a badly written thriller have in common? With both, you know what's going to happen next.

"Tell us, when will these things be, and what will be the sign of your coming and of the end of the age?" And Jesus answered them, "See that no one leads you astray. For many will come in my name, saying, 'I am the Christ,' and they will lead many astray. And you will hear of wars and rumors of wars. See that you are not alarmed, for this must take place, but the end is not yet. For nation will rise against nation, and kingdom against kingdom, and there will be famines and earthquakes in various places. All these are but the beginning of the birth pains."

Matthew 24:3b- 8

#160

Who is the first person to read a new book? The author. It's impossible for the writer to write without reading.

And I saw a strong angel proclaiming with a loud voice, "Who is worthy to open the scroll and break its seals?" And they sang a new song, saying, "Worthy are you to take the scroll and to open its seals, for you were slain, and by your blood you ransomed people for God from every tribe and language and people and nation, and you have made them a kingdom and priests to our God, and they shall reign on the earth."

Revelation 5:2, 9- 10

#161

Is it a great accolade for a movie to be honored as, "One of the best movies of the year," on January 1st?

God called the light Day, and the darkness he called Night. And there was evening and there was morning, the first day.

Genesis 1:5

#162

When situations seem suspicious we say, "Something smells fishy." What would someone say when things seem suspect at a fish market, since it already smells fishy there?

And the Lord appointed a great fish to swallow up Jonah. And Jonah was in the belly of the fish three days and three nights.

Jonah 1:17

#163

Why is an adult who rides a bicycle to work in a rural area seen as poor, while a person who does the same in a big city is seen as environmentally-conscious?

O kingdoms of the earth, sing to God; sing praises to the Lord, Selah to him who rides in the heavens, the ancient heavens; behold, he sends out his voice, his mighty voice.

Psalm 68:32- 33

#164

Don't you think solar farms are a *bright* idea?

And I saw the holy city, new Jerusalem, coming down out of heaven from God, prepared as a bride adorned for her husband. And the city has no need of sun or moon to shine on it, for the glory of God gives it light, and its lamp is the Lamb.

Revelation 21:2, 23

#165

What do you call a security person at an inflatable attraction who throws out all unruly jumpers? A bouncer.

"Blessed are you when people hate you and when they exclude you and revile you and spurn your name as evil, on account of the Son of Man! Rejoice in that day, and leap for joy, for behold, your reward is great in heaven; for so their fathers did to the prophets."

Luke 6:22-23

#166

If the weather was the same every day, wouldn't the weather show on TV be a perpetual re-run?

"Oh, I've seen this weather before."

And the Pharisees and Sadducees came, and to test him they asked him to show them a sign from heaven. He answered them, "When it is evening, you say, 'It will be fair weather, for the sky is red.' And in the morning, 'It will be stormy today, for the sky is red and threatening.' You know how to interpret the appearance of the sky, but you cannot interpret the signs of the times. An evil and adulterous generation seeks for a sign, but no sign will be given to it except the sign of Jonah." So he left them and departed.

Matthew 16:1- 4

End of the Cruise

For one year I made my nest inside the belly of the
wooden vessel.

Noah called me to service and sent me out through
the portal for reconnaissance.

It felt good to stretch my feathers wide and pump my
stiff wings.

I flew across the expanse, the reflection of my form
visible on the surface below.

The earth was covered with water because of its
inability to swim.

It lay at the bottom of the ocean like sunken treasure
waiting to be brought to the surface.

I flew over the world-wide ocean until my strength
was exhausted, no place to land.

Back to the floating island to rest my wings from their
unaccustomed flight.

For one week I went on leave waiting for flight orders
to come from my superior.

Once again, I stretched forth my wings setting an
unknown course into the clean sky

Surrounded by God's most used color.

A great distance I flew, finding at last a landing pad of green.

I sat in a tree for the first time in months while scanning for other signs of flora.

With a plucked leaf from the olive tree I flew peaceably back to home base.

I carried my green cargo through the blue world to the last of earth's sailors.

A week later I went out to explore the uninhabited, resurrected world.

I no longer saw my reflection below me for the water was gone.

Other hues emerged from the former one-color planet.

Greens, browns, and grays brought back memories of the pre-flood world.

I was glad that God had chosen me to be on his ship's manifest.

But now I am eager to keep my wings in flight across this world of new growth.

I am forever glad to leave my sea legs behind.

#167

Why do people who hate coffee still own coffee tables?

A dispute also arose among them, as to which of them was to be regarded as the greatest. "For who is the greater, one who reclines at table or one who serves? Is it not the one who reclines at table? But I am among you as the one who serves."

Luke 22:24, 27

#168

Why is *microscopic* such a huge word?

And he said, "With what can we compare the kingdom of God, or what parable shall we use for it? It is like a grain of mustard seed, which, when sown on the ground, is the smallest of all the seeds on earth, yet when it is sown it grows up and becomes larger than all the garden plants and puts out large branches, so that the birds of the air can make nests in its shade."

Mark 4:30- 32

#169

We call an inactive person who lays on the couch eating potato chips a couch potato. What would you call someone who lies on a couch and eats pickles? A couch cucumber?

How long will you lie there, O sluggard? When will you arise from your sleep? A little sleep, a little slumber, a little folding of the hands to rest, and poverty will come upon you like a robber, and want like an armed man.

Proverbs 6:9-11

#170

Aren't you glad there are people who take a stand for their values? I'm glad there are stand-up comedians. We need people who are willing to stand up on the behalf of comedy, and defend the rights of the people to smile, laugh, and joke around.

Open your mouth for the mute, for the rights of all who are destitute. Open your mouth, judge righteously, defend the rights of the poor and needy.

Proverbs 31:8- 9

#171

Do we build birdbaths because birds are *fowl* smelling?

If the whole body were an eye, where would be the sense of hearing? If the whole body were an ear, where would be the sense of smell? But as it is, God arranged the members in the body, each one of them, as he chose. Now you are the body of Christ and individually members of it.

1 Corinthians 12:17- 18, 27

#172

When someone is afraid to take a dare, we call them chicken. What do chickens call each other in that same situation?

"O Jerusalem, Jerusalem, the city that kills the prophets and stones those who are sent to it! How often would I have gathered your children together as a hen gathers her brood under her wings, and you would not!"

Luke 13:34

#173

Don't you think we should build more wind farms? When I first heard of them, the concept blew me away.

Then a wind from the Lord sprang up, and it brought quail from the sea and let them fall beside the camp, about a day's journey on this side and a day's journey on the other side, around the camp, and about two cubits above the ground. And the people rose all that day and all night and all the next day, and gathered the quail. Those who gathered least gathered ten homers. And they spread them out for themselves all around the camp.

Numbers 11:31- 32

#174

Were motorcycles made for people who hate to pedal, but still want to ride a bike?

"You shall not hate your brother in your heart, but you shall reason frankly with your neighbor, lest you incur sin because of him."

Leviticus 19:17

#175

Did you know I have been troubled lately? I have been worried that I will start to worry.

Humble yourselves, therefore, under the mighty hand of God so that at the proper time he may exalt you, casting all your anxieties on him, because he cares for you.

1 Peter 5:6- 7

#176

When people ask when I last ate, do I tell them the time when I started to eat, or when I finished? Please help me—I don't know what information to feed them.

So, whether you eat or drink, or whatever you do, do all to the glory of God.

1 Corinthians 10:31

#177

Do you think people would be more inclined to rake the lawn in autumn if money grew on trees? Those motivated to do yard work could really rake in the cash!

Then the angel showed me the river of the water of life, bright as crystal, flowing from the throne of God and of the Lamb through the middle of the street of the city; also, on either side of the river, the tree of life with its twelve kinds of fruit, yielding its fruit each month. The leaves of the tree were for the healing of the nations.

Revelation 22:1- 2

#178

I just saw a sign that had an illustration of a handgun with a X drawn over it. I know X means hug, so does the sign mean we are to hug guns?

For everything there is a season, and a time for every matter under heaven: a time to embrace, and a time to refrain from embracing;

Ecclesiastes 3:1, 5b

#179

Ducking is what ducks should do more often when they are shot at during duck season. Don't you think they would live longer if they lived up to their name?

And Saul hurled the spear, for he thought, "I will pin David to the wall." But David evaded him twice. Saul was afraid of David because the Lord was with him but had departed from Saul.

1 Samuel 18:11- 12

#180

Do you know why I don't want to be a window cleaner? I'm afraid someone will ask me to remove the stain from stained glass windows.

Bring the full tithe into the storehouse, that there may be food in my house. And thereby put me to the test, says the Lord of hosts, if I will not open the windows of heaven for you and pour down for you a blessing until there is no more need.

Malachi 3:10

#181

Why was my mother upset when I put my crystal rocks on our dining table when we had some important guests over for dinner? She'd told me, "Put out the fine crystal." I promise they were the best I had.

Blessed is everyone who fears the Lord, who walks in his ways! Your wife will be like a fruitful vine within your house; your children will be like olive shoots around your table.

Psalm 128:1, 3

#182

Do you think junk collectors receive more junk mail than the average person?

Therefore do not throw away your confidence, which has a great reward. For you have need of endurance, so that when you have done the will of God you may receive what is promised.

Hebrews 10:35- 36

#183

Why do we have the term litterbug? I have never seen bugs littering, but I have seen a lot of humans throwing trash on the ground. It really bugs me when I see people litter. They're a bunch of pollution pests.

Indeed, I count everything as loss because of the surpassing worth of knowing Christ Jesus my Lord. For his sake I have suffered the loss of all things and count them as rubbish, in order that I may gain Christ.

Philippians 3:8

#184

Do you know why I couldn't attend the Liar's Club meetings? They kept telling me the wrong time for their gatherings.

Who is the liar but he who denies that Jesus is the Christ? This is the antichrist, he who denies the Father and the Son.

1 John 2:22

#185

Are megaphones used for phoning people that are hard-of-hearing?

And when the men had come to him, they said, "John the Baptist has sent us to you, saying, 'Are you the one who is to come, or shall we look for another?'" And he answered them, "Go and tell John what you have seen and heard: the blind receive their sight, the lame walk, lepers are cleansed, and the deaf hear, the dead are raised up, the poor have good news preached to them."

Luke 7:20, 22

#186

Did you know that on earth, streets of gold wouldn't make winter driving conditions golden?

And the twelve gates (of New Jerusalem) were twelve pearls, each of the gates made of a single pearl, and the street of the city was pure gold, like transparent glass.

Revelation 21:21

#187

Did you know that a gravedigger doesn't have to dig his own grave? His boss lets him off to rest in peace.

He was oppressed, and he was afflicted, yet he opened not his mouth; like a lamb that is led to the slaughter, and like a sheep that before its shearers is silent, so he opened not his mouth. And they made his grave with the wicked and with a rich man in his death, although he had done no violence, and there was no deceit in his mouth.

Isaiah 53:7, 9

#188

Did you know that *reptile* is not a type of ceramic flooring used in the chamber of the House of Representatives?

"Behold, I am sending you out as sheep in the midst of wolves, so be wise as serpents and innocent as doves."

Matthew 10:16

Living Memories

Our loved ones have died

But our memories of them will never die

Our memories have not been buried

In a casket, twelve feet below our thoughts

Nor cremated, so our cherished times with them

Cannot flicker and burn

We are separated from our dear ones,

But they live on

They dwell in our musing

Regularly, they come to our consciousness

Summoned by a sight, sound, or smell

They are alive and well in our thinking

A living memorial erected in our minds

#189

At the end of dictator school, how long do the students remain in an internship position before they become certified dictators? It depends on how long it takes them to oust the current leader under which they are interning.

Shepherd the flock of God that is among you, exercising oversight, not under compulsion, but willingly, as God would have you; not for shameful gain, but eagerly; not domineering over those in your charge, but being examples to the flock.

1 Peter 5:2- 3

#190

Why do so many people want us to talk about underwear on their voicemail? At least, I assume that is what's meant by "A brief message."

And David danced before the Lord with all his might. And David was wearing a linen ephod.

2 Samuel 6:14

#191

Did you know that corrupt leaders are very handy with a broom? They are always trying to sweep their illegal dealings under the rug.

For nothing is hidden that will not be made manifest, nor is anything secret that will not be known and come to light.

Luke 8:17

#192

To give someone *the skinny* is to give them the confidential facts on a topic or person. To *chew the fat* is defined as gossiping or informal conversation. Is it possible to chew the fat about the skinny?

And Pharaoh said to Joseph, "Say to your brothers, Do this: load your beasts and go back to the land of Canaan, and take your father and your households, and come to me, and I will give you the best of the land of Egypt, and you shall eat the fat of the land."

Genesis 45:17- 18

#193

What does it mean to have equal rights in a dystopian society? It means all people will not be refused the right to experience unpleasant and bad things.

"And he called out, 'Father Abraham, have mercy on me, and send Lazarus to dip the end of his finger in water and cool my tongue, for I am in anguish in this flame.' But Abraham said, 'Child, remember that you in your lifetime received your good things, and Lazarus in like manner bad things; but now he is comforted here, and you are in anguish.'"

Luke 16:24- 25

#194

Why are they called *freeways* when they're so expensive to build?

A voice cries: "In the wilderness prepare the way of the Lord; make straight in the desert a highway for our God. Every valley shall be lifted up, and every mountain and hill be made low."

Isaiah 40:3- 4b

#195

Would you like a good hygiene tip? When you finish your paperwork in the bathroom, you should never leave a paper trail.

"You shall have a place outside the camp, and you shall go out to it. And you shall have a trowel with your tools, and when you sit down outside, you shall dig a hole with it and turn back and cover up your excrement. Because the Lord your God walks in the midst of your camp, to deliver you and to give up your enemies before you, therefore your camp must be holy, so that he may not see anything indecent among you and turn away from you."

Deuteronomy 23:12- 14

#196

Do you find it odd that people still get goosebumps in countries where there are no geese?

Look at the birds of the air: they neither sow nor reap nor gather into barns, and yet your heavenly Father feeds them. Are you not of more value than they?

Matthew 6:26

#197

When someone is lost, people form a search party. Why are they having a party when someone is missing?

And Jesus said to him, "Today salvation has come to this house, since he also is a son of Abraham. For the Son of Man came to seek and to save the lost."

Luke 19:9- 10

#198

Would you like to be able to turn in a shorter college thesis? If we can get educational institutions to change from page numbers to page letters, then your thesis would be a lot shorter. In English, we could only have twenty-six pages.

I had much to write to you, but I would rather not write with pen and ink. I hope to see you soon, and we will talk face to face.

3 John 13- 14

#199

To have a feather in your cap means to have a success or accomplishment that you are proud of. I don't see a lot of people wearing feathers in their caps. Is that because a lot of people aren't succeeding these days, or is it that birds are stingier with their feathers than they used to be?

He will cover you with his pinions, and under his wings you will find refuge; his faithfulness is a shield and buckler.

Psalm 91:4

#200

Is it true that pirates don't star in most pirated movies?

When they saw the star, they rejoiced exceedingly with great joy. And going into the house, they saw the child with Mary his mother, and they fell down and worshiped him. Then, opening their treasures, they offered him gifts, gold and frankincense and myrrh.

Matthew 2:10- 11

#201

People say, "Never give up!" Does that mean we should always give down?

You, however, have followed my teaching, my conduct, my aim in life, my faith, my patience, my love, my steadfastness.

2 Timothy 3:10

#202

Is *stopwatch* another way to say *broken watch*?

At that time Joshua spoke to the Lord in the day when the Lord gave the Amorites over to the sons of Israel, and he said in the sight of Israel, "Sun, stand still at Gibeon, and moon, in the Valley of Aijalon." And the sun stood still, and the moon stopped, until the nation took vengeance on their enemies.

Joshua 10:12- 13

#203

Why do people have butterflies in their stomachs when they are nervous? I suppose the more nervous you are, the more butterflies you will have. Could you have so many butterflies in your stomach that you would be able to fly?

For many, of whom I have often told you and now tell you even with tears, walk as enemies of the cross of Christ. Their end is destruction, their god is their belly, and they glory in their shame, with minds set on earthly things.

Philippians 3:18-19

#204

Did you know that some people religiously practice a good habit, while others also wear one religiously?

Religion that is pure and undefiled before God the Father is this: to visit orphans and widows in their affliction, and to keep oneself unstained from the world.

James 1:27

#205

Are mothballs manufactured for moth sports? Put mothballs in your closet and say to the moths, "Play ball!"

"Do not lay up for yourselves treasures on earth, where moth and rust destroy and where thieves break in and steal, but lay up for yourselves treasures in heaven, where neither moth nor rust destroys and where thieves do not break in and steal."

Matthew 6:19- 20

#206

What is your view on non-stop flights? A lot of people think non-stop flights are great, but I like to eventually land and get off the plane.

Fear and trembling come upon me, and horror overwhelms me. And I say, "Oh, that I had wings like a dove! I would fly away and be at rest;"

Psalm 55:5- 6

Future Visit

The future is hidden from me,
Concerning when alongside you I'll be.

All I have in my possession is today,
And you live so very far away.

One thing I know is true,
If I begin my journey now, I say with sorrow,
I will not be able to reach you,
Until this day is past, and it's tomorrow.

#207

Why do the police always give us a quiz when they pull us over?

Police Quiz Question #1:

"Do you know why I pulled you over?"

Wrong Reply to this Question:

"Is this question going to be on the final exam?"

Let every person be subject to the governing authorities. For there is no authority except from God, and those that exist have been instituted by God.

Romans 13:1

#208

Are people on-the-fence because they are off-the-wall?

For God alone my soul waits in silence; from him comes my salvation. He alone is my rock and my salvation, my fortress; I shall not be greatly shaken. How long will all of you attack a man to batter him, like a leaning wall, a tottering fence?

Psalm 62:1- 3

#209

If everyone spoke in contract law language, would contracts then be written in normal English?

Is the law then contrary to the promises of God? Certainly not! For if a law had been given that could give life, then righteousness would indeed be by the law. But the Scripture imprisoned everything under sin, so that the promise by faith in Jesus Christ might be given to those who believe.

Galatians 3:21- 22

#210

To call someone *la-di-da* means they are snobbish. When la-di-da precedes do, re, mi, what does it mean? It means a snobby singer.

Do nothing from selfish ambition or conceit, but in humility count others more significant than yourselves.

Philippians 2:3

#211

Do you know what *spelunk* means? Spelunk is the sound spelunkers make when they fall from a rope onto the cave floor while spelunking.

And what more shall I say? For time would fail me to tell of Gideon, Barak, Samson, Jephthah, of David and Samuel and the prophets—who through faith conquered kingdoms, enforced justice, obtained promises, stopped the mouths of lions, quenched the power of fire, escaped the edge of the sword, were made strong out of weakness, became mighty in war, put foreign armies to flight. They were stoned, they were sawn in two, they were killed with the sword. They went about in skins of sheep and goats, destitute, afflicted, mistreated—of whom the world was not worthy—wandering about in deserts and mountains, and in dens and caves of the earth.

Hebrews 11:32- 34, 37- 38

#212

Having unlimited minutes on your teleportation device is important. You don't want to run out of minutes in the middle of a teleportation session, because you are on a limited plan.

"Hello, can you see me now?"

And he commanded the chariot to stop, and they both went down into the water, Philip and the eunuch, and he baptized him. And when they came up out of the water, the Spirit of the Lord carried Philip away, and the eunuch saw him no more, and went on his way rejoicing. But Philip found himself at Azotus, and as he passed through he preached the gospel to all the towns until he came to Caesarea.

Acts 8:38- 40

#213

Don't you think shooting stars should be illegal? If people shoot too many stars, it will be a lot darker at night. Put your gun on safety and watch the beautiful stars.

He determines the number of the stars; he gives to all of them their names.

Psalm 147:4

#214

Why do so many people own sneakers, but so few of them sneak on a regular basis?

Be sober-minded; be watchful. Your adversary the devil prowls around like a roaring lion, seeking someone to devour.

1 Peter 5:8

#215

People say hugs are healthy. If that's true, why did I lose my breath and pass out when I was bear-hugged by the wrestler Ivan the Giant?

"I will arise and go to my father, and I will say to him, Father, I have sinned against heaven and before you. I am no longer worthy to be called your son. Treat me as one of your hired servants." And he arose and came to his father. But while he was still a long way off, his father saw him and felt compassion, and ran and embraced him and kissed him.

Luke 15:18- 20

#216

A bookmark is used to mark a person's place in a book. Is a watermark used to mark where a person stopped swimming during their last swim session?

Your eyes saw my unformed substance; in your book were written, every one of them, the days that were formed for me, when as yet there was none of them.

Psalm 139:16

#217

Can you define plates, cups, and bowls? A concise definition of all three is as follows: plates, cups, and bowls are all cabinet members that don't possess the power to vote each other out of the cabinet during a disagreement concerning proper table place-setting rules.

I will lift up the cup of salvation and call on the name of the Lord, I will pay my vows to the Lord in the presence of all his people.

Psalm 116:13- 14

#218

Can you define the word archery?
archery, arch·ery: n. the sport of shooting arrows at arches with a bow that is curved to resemble what it shoots at.

Come, behold the works of the Lord, how he has brought desolations on the earth. He makes wars cease to the end of the earth; he breaks the bow and shatters the spear.

Psalm 46:8- 9a

Rescued

He staggered through the desert of physical pleasures.
Past many dry and dusty possessions he stumbled.
He thirsted for something deeper that contained true
meaning.
He yearned for what would truly satisfy his longings.
Through the stale existence of temporary enjoyment
He steadily regressed from haze to murky black, and
then into nefarious darkness.
Unexpectedly, a bright light shown from heaven
Invading all of his pathetic earthly being.
The warmth of the light generated understanding
In the depths of his crusty and dead soul.
He realized that all he possessed was refuse at best.
What he needed was true life.
True knowledge took residence in his mind and heart
As he pledged absolute allegiance to the Father of
light.
Though he lived and moved in the same old dark and
gloomy land,
He walked in brilliant light, dispersing it to those who
reside in the dominion of doom.
He rejoiced, full of thankfulness and gratitude toward
the one
Who found him in the deep, dark bottom of the well
of death.

#219

Do you keep up with what is popular in prison reading material? The magazine Prison Weekly just published their top book recommendations for the year.

1. Cell-Mate to Check-Mate: From Prisoner to Chess Master—The Story of Big Bad Bob
2. Thinking Outside Your Cell: 101 Ways to Escape Prison Mentally
3. New Kids on the Cell-Block: Biography of a Juvenile Prison Band
4. Orange is Out: Fresh Prison Fashions
5. Jail Aerobics: New Prison Work-out Methods that Will Help You Break-out of Your Routine

I therefore, a prisoner for the Lord, urge you to walk in a manner worthy of the calling to which you have been called, with all humility and gentleness, with patience, bearing with one another in love, eager to maintain the unity of the Spirit in the bond of peace.

Ephesians 4:1- 3

#220

Don't you wish you had more liquid assets? I am going to the river to borrow money. They have banks on each side that run the entire length of the waterway. With those enormous banks, I think they will be able to float me a loan.

"And on the banks, on both sides of the river, there will grow all kinds of trees for food. Their leaves will not wither, nor their fruit fail, but they will bear fresh fruit every month, because the water for them flows from the sanctuary. Their fruit will be for food, and their leaves for healing."

Ezekiel 47:12

#221

Why do people call me lazy? There are a lot of things I like about work. I like break time, lunch time, quitting time, and pay day.

A slack hand causes poverty, but the hand of the diligent makes rich.

Proverbs 10:4

#222

Why do people get so defensive whey they are told they need to take a defensive driving class? I guess they do have a point. The fact that they were defensive concerning the need to take a defensive driving class does show that they are probably already defensive enough.

Then he sent out a second horseman, who came to them and said, "Thus the king has said, 'Is it peace?'" And Jehu answered, "What do you have to do with peace? Turn around and ride behind me." Again the watchman reported, "He reached them, but he is not coming back. And the driving is like the driving of Jehu the son of Nimshi, for he drives furiously."

2 Kings 9:19- 20

#223

The definition of a scarecrow is very strict. A scarecrow is a model of a person dressed in old clothes and put in a field to scare away the crows. Would the crows call our bluff if the scarecrow was dressed in a business suit?

Crow Leader to his Crow Cronies: "Hey boys, that's not a real farmer! No one works in the fields in a suit and tie. Clearly, the corn field is open for crow business, because no human is guarding the field."

Those who sow in tears shall reap with shouts of joy! He who goes out weeping, bearing the seed for sowing, shall come home with shouts of joy, bringing his sheaves with him.

Psalm 126:5- 6

#224

Do you know why people like to write their names in wet cement? I'm no psychologist, but I think they're trying to cement their name in history.

You are fellow citizens with the saints and members of the household of God, built on the foundation of the apostles and prophets, Christ Jesus himself being the cornerstone,

Ephesians 2:19a- 20

#225

Have you ever heard someone say the following statement? "I wish I was where I am in my life right now when I was young." If that were the case, then they would be a young person with a lot of injuries and ailments.

The glory of young men is their strength, but the splendor of old men is their gray hair.

Proverbs 20:29

#226

Sometimes people say, "Just roll the dice." They mean that there's a chance the decision we're making might result in a fortunate outcome, and we should take the risk. Wouldn't I have a better shot at rolling the dice if they were round?

When the soldiers had crucified Jesus, they took his garments and divided them into four parts, one part for each soldier; also his tunic. But the tunic was seamless, woven in one piece from top to bottom, so they said to one another, "Let us not tear it, but cast lots for it to see whose it shall be."

John 19:23- 24a

#227

Palindromes are words that are spelled the same forward and backward. Do you know some simple palindrome words? Examples of the simplest palindromes are the words *a* and *I*.

"I am the Alpha and the Omega, the first and the last, the beginning and the end."

Revelation 22:13

Resurrection

Because of the resurrection of Jesus, we can have a relationship with him.

Because of the resurrection of Jesus, this relationship will never end.

#228

Why do people so often say, "It doesn't hurt to try," in connection with starting something new? That was not my experience when I took ultimate fighting classes. It does hurt to try.

And he who was seated on the throne said, "Behold, I am making all things new." Also he said, "Write this down, for these words are trustworthy and true."

Revelation 21:5

#229

If people say they are going to "foil their plans" when they want to spoil someone's activities, what do I say if I just want to mess with someone's plans a little, but still want them to see through my prank? Maybe, "cellophane their plans"?

The Lord brings the counsel of the nations to nothing; he frustrates the plans of the peoples.

Psalm 33:10

#230

Do you believe in magic carpets? I think magic carpets are a myth. Carpets get very dirty and must be cleaned. I have never seen a magic carpet cleaner business. Since magic carpet cleaners don't exist, neither do magic carpets; unless all the magic carpets are extremely dirty. If they are that dirty, I wouldn't ride on them anyway.

A writing of Hezekiah king of Judah, after he had been sick and had recovered from his sickness:
I said, "I shall not see the Lord, the Lord in the land of the living; I shall look on man no more among the inhabitants of the world. My dwelling is plucked up and removed from me like a shepherd's tent; like a weaver I have rolled up my life; he cuts me off from the loom; from day to night you bring me to an end;"

Isaiah 38:9, 11- 12

#231

Has anyone ever underestimated your abilities?
Sometimes people think I don't have a lot of skills.
They tell me, "You can't cut the mustard."
I tell them, "Yes I can, but I like my mustard
unsliced."

*Let no one despise you for your youth, but set the
believers an example in speech, in conduct, in love, in
faith, in purity.*

1 Timothy 4:12

#232

The four heating elements on top of the stove are
called burners. Isn't that a red flag that I will probably
overcook my food?

*Then from the sacrifice of the peace offering he shall
offer as a food offering to the Lord its fat; he shall
remove the whole fat tail, cut off close to the
backbone, and the fat that covers the entrails and all
the fat that is on the entrails. And the priest shall
burn it on the altar as a food offering to the LORD.*

Leviticus 3:9, 11

#233

Whatever happened to the noble idea of keeping your word? Before the invention of paper, contracts were written in stone. It was a time when people kept their word more faithfully. Back then, it was harder to break a contract. Sometimes you had to smash it on the ground several times before it broke.

If a man vows a vow to the Lord, or swears an oath to bind himself by a pledge, he shall not break his word. He shall do according to all that proceeds out of his mouth.

Numbers 30:2

#234

Can you define napkin?

Napkin, nap·kin: n. a short duration of sleep taken by one of your elderly relatives during a meal at the dinner table.

"You shall stand up before the gray head and honor the face of an old man, and you shall fear your God: I am the Lord."

Leviticus 19:32

#235

Do you know the main function for headphones? People say they wear headphones so they won't disturb other people in public when listening to music. That might be true, but I've seen a lot people using headphones in public so they won't hear how bad they sound when they sing out loud.

Make a joyful noise to the Lord, all the earth; break forth into joyous song and sing praises!

Psalm 98:4

#236

Did you know that sometimes, being the owner of a water bed is just another way to say you have a leaky roof?

A foolish son is ruin to his father, and a wife's quarreling is a continual dripping of rain.

Proverbs 19:13

#237

Did you know that a lot of robbers grow facial hair? Razor wire on the top of fences is a constant reminder that there are plenty of criminals out there who don't want a close shave.

But the princes of the Ammonites said to Hanun their lord, "Do you think, because David has sent comforters to you, that he is honoring your father? Has not David sent his servants to you to search the city and to spy it out and to overthrow it?" So Hanun took David's servants and shaved off half the beard of each and cut off their garments in the middle, at their hips, and sent them away. When it was told to David, he sent to meet them, for the men were greatly ashamed. And the king said, "Remain at Jericho until your beards have grown and then return."

2 Samuel 10:3- 5

#238

The doctor told me to elevate my legs more often to reduce swelling. That's why I take multiple elevator rides every day to elevate my legs. It's not helping the swelling in my legs, but I have met a lot of people, and because of that my circle of friends did swell. Why would the doctor tell me to do something that would increase swelling?

Forty years you sustained them in the wilderness, and they lacked nothing. Their clothes did not wear out and their feet did not swell.

Nehemiah 9:21

#239

A barista is a person who makes and serves coffee. Therefore, shouldn't a person who makes and serves alcoholic drinks be called a *coffeeshopista*?

And do not get drunk with wine, for that is debauchery, but be filled with the Spirit.

Ephesians 5:18

#240

Is there anything positive about a traffic jam? Yes, a traffic jam gives people enough time to eat their toast in their car during the morning commute. Toast and jam!

After this I looked, and behold, a great multitude that no one could number, from every nation, from all tribes and peoples and languages, standing before the throne and before the Lamb, clothed in white robes, with palm branches in their hands, and crying out with a loud voice, "Salvation belongs to our God who sits on the throne, and to the Lamb!"

Revelation 7:9- 10

#241

Horses are good at creating transportation art. Haven't you ever heard of a horse-drawn carriage?

Some trust in chariots and some in horses, but we trust in the name of the Lord our God.

Psalm 20:7

#242

When we experience difficulties people frequently say, "When the world gives you lemons, make lemonade." Why does the world give people so many lemons? If the world would occasionally give people limes, they could change things up and make limeade.

And God said, "Behold, I have given you every plant yielding seed that is on the face of all the earth, and every tree with seed in its fruit. You shall have them for food."

Genesis 1:29

#243

Are you successful in your life? I haven't found the key to success yet. I can't even find my car keys.

This Book of the Law shall not depart from your mouth, but you shall meditate on it day and night, so that you may be careful to do according to all that is written in it. For then you will make your way prosperous, and then you will have good success.

Joshua 1:8

#244

Have you noticed more difficulties in your life as you grow older? One of the problems with growing old is the increased number of arguments you have. The mind tells the body to do something, and the body wants to argue about it.

What causes quarrels and what causes fights among you? Is it not this, that your passions are at war within you?

James 4:1

#245

Do you know why a lot of great stories in books are hidden from us? It's because they are kept under cover.

"For if you believed Moses, you would believe me; for he wrote of me. But if you do not believe his writings, how will you believe my words?"

John 5:46- 47

#246

Have you ever heard of the music genre fragrant rock? There's a new fragrant rock band named Potpourri. They pride themselves in making aromatic sounds, but so far, all the music reviews say they stink.

For we are the aroma of Christ to God among those who are being saved and among those who are perishing, to one a fragrance from death to death, to the other a fragrance from life to life.

2 Corinthians 2:15- 16a

#247

A vigil held next to the body of a person who has died is called a wake. Doesn't it make more sense to call this vigil *not awake*?

Awake, my glory! Awake, O harp and lyre! I will awake the dawn! I will give thanks to you, O Lord, among the peoples; I will sing praises to you among the nations.

Psalm 57:8- 9

#248

Do you own a brief case? Most people use brief cases incorrectly. A brief case is a small bag used for carrying underwear during a short trip.

"You shall make for them linen undergarments to cover their naked flesh. They shall reach from hips to the thigh; and they shall be on Aaron and on his sons when they go into the tent of meeting or when they come near the altar to minister in the Holy Place, lest they bear guilt and die. This shall be a statute forever for him and for his offspring after him."

Exodus 28:42- 43

#249

What is the definition of a fruit stand?

fruit stand: v. when fruit takes a firm stand on issues dealing with fruit consumption

But the fruit of the Spirit is love, joy, peace, patience, kindness, goodness, faithfulness, gentleness, self-control; against such things there is no law.

Galatians 5:22- 23

#250

Have you ever heard parents tell their children, "Don't run with scissors!"? This saying originated decades ago when track relay teams passed scissors to each other during a race. After a terrible exchange occurred during a major track meet, the National Athletic Committee adopted the slogan, "Don't run with scissors!" Shortly thereafter, batons were introduced in place of scissors, and the number of paramedics that were required during a track meet was dramatically reduced.

I have fought the good fight, I have finished the race, I have kept the faith.

2 Timothy 4:7

#251

Did you know that travel mugs have existed since the beginning of mankind? Travel mugs are the facial expressions people make during their travels.

And he said to them, "Go into all the world and proclaim the gospel to the whole creation."

Mark 16:15

#252

Do you regularly try to reach your optimum effort in your tasks? I am afraid to reach the pinnacle of my performance, because I know it's all downhill from there.

And whatever you do, in word or deed, do everything in the name of the Lord Jesus, giving thanks to God the Father through him.

Colossians 3:17

#253

Have you ever met a book that was quiet? Me neither. They always have something to say.

For the word of God is living and active, sharper than any two-edged sword, piercing to the division of soul and of spirit, of joints and of marrow, and discerning the thoughts and intentions of the heart.

Hebrews 4:12

#254

When we are awake and have a problem, people tell us, "Don't lose sleep over it," which is another way of saying not to worry about it. Isn't not losing sleep and losing wake the same thing?

My son, do not lose sight of these—keep sound wisdom and discretion, and they will be life for your soul and adornment for your neck. Then you will walk on your way securely, and your foot will not stumble. If you lie down, you will not be afraid; when you lie down, your sleep will be sweet.

Proverbs 3:21- 24

#255

Shouldn't it be required for all tunnels to have a light installed at the end of them? That way people will always be able to see the light at the end of the tunnel.

Again Jesus spoke to them, saying, "I am the light of the world. Whoever follows me will not walk in darkness, but will have the light of life."

John 8:12

#256

When people play hide and seek with me and leave out the seek part, are they trying to send me a message concerning our relationship?

Set your minds on things that are above, not on things that are on earth. For you have died, and your life is hidden with Christ in God.

Colossians 3:2- 3

#257

Is there something that you are good at? I don't like to brag, but I'm really good at un-parallel parking in a parallel parking spot.

But far be it from me to boast except in the cross of our Lord Jesus Christ, by which the world has been crucified to me, and I to the world.

Galatians 6:14

#258

Do you know why people came up with the idea for wooden shoes? Wooden shoes were invented by the Dutch in their attempt to walk on water.

The sea became rough because a strong wind was blowing. When they had rowed about three or four miles, they saw Jesus walking on the sea and coming near the boat, and they were frightened. But he said to them, "It is I; do not be afraid."

John 6:18- 20

#259

Have you ever been given faulty cheese? I received some defective Swiss cheese once. It didn't have holes in it.

Your hands fashioned and made me, and now you have destroyed me altogether. Remember that you have made me like clay; and will you return me to the dust? Did you not pour me out like milk and curdle me like cheese?

Job 10:8- 10

#260

Have you found that books are not afraid to speak? We should be more like books: have a spine and speak what's inside. Are we on the same page concerning being book-like?

If I say, "I will not mention him, or speak any more in his name," there is in my heart as it were a burning fire shut up in my bones, and I am weary with holding it in, and I cannot.

Jeremiah 20:9

#261

Did you know that the words of a book do not believe in gray areas? Yes, they live in a black and white world.

Woe to those who call evil good and good evil, who put darkness for light and light for darkness, who put bitter for sweet and sweet for bitter!

Isaiah 5:20

#262

Every state in the U.S. has a capital city and a capitol building. Why don't they also have lower-case buildings?

"Since the day that I brought my people out of the land of Egypt, I chose no city out of all the tribes of Israel in which to build a house, that my name might be there, and I chose no man as prince over my people Israel; but I have chosen Jerusalem that my name may be there, and I have chosen David to be over my people Israel."

2 Chronicles 6:5- 6

#263

Shouldn't people who work from home buy stationary bikes? That way they could commute back and forth to work in an environmentally-friendly way.

The Lord God took the man and put him in the garden of Eden to work it and keep it.

Genesis 2:15

#264

A lot of people make a toast at gatherings to celebrate some great event or accomplishment. When people throw a party to celebrate a financial blessing because they have made a lot of bread, can they use any bread to toast this monetary advancement, or should it only be pumpernickel?

Jesus said to them, "I am the bread of life; whoever comes to me shall not hunger, and whoever believes in me shall never thirst."

John 6:35

#265

Did Baker Bob come into a lot of dough? He must have, because he built a new high-rise apartment building named Yeast Towers.

He told them another parable. "The kingdom of heaven is like leaven that a woman took and hid in three measures of flour, till it was all leavened."

Matthew 13:33

#266

Non-verbal language is the first language that a child learns in every country. A newborn is greeted by a butt-spanking from the doctor—somewhat cruel first words, don't you think?

"Truly, truly, I say to you, you will weep and lament, but the world will rejoice. You will be sorrowful, but your sorrow will turn into joy. When a woman is giving birth, she has sorrow because her hour has come, but when she has delivered the baby, she no longer remembers the anguish, for joy that a human being has been born into the world. So also you have sorrow now, but I will see you again, and your hearts will rejoice, and no one will take your joy from you."

John 16:20- 22

#267

Sometimes the problem is not that people are hard of hearing, but that the speakers are soft of speaking. Did I write that loud enough?

A soft answer turns away wrath, but a harsh word stirs up anger.

Proverbs 15:1

#268

Do you think it was a bad idea to use the fresh-cut grass scented air-freshener at the allergy clinic?

As for man, his days are like grass; he flourishes like a flower of the field; for the wind passes over it, and it is gone, and its place knows it no more.

Psalm 103:15- 16

Few

Smoke that is drifting away

Green grass that has wilted

A shadow stretched to its extreme

The days of a man are few

#269

Did you know that "the day that time stood still" really happened? That was the day my watch battery died.

For the wages of sin is death, but the free gift of God is eternal life in Christ Jesus our Lord.

Romans 6:23

#270

Don't work-outs sometimes feel the same as being worked-over?

For while bodily training is of some value, godliness is of value in every way, as it holds promise for the present life and also for the life to come.

1 Timothy 4:8

#271

Do you know what an amnesiac and an illiterate person have in common? Both cannot write their name.

The one who conquers, I will make him a pillar in the temple of my God. Never shall he go out of it, and I will write on him the name of my God, and the name of the city of my God, the new Jerusalem, which comes down from my God out of heaven, and my own new name.

Revelation 3:12

#272

Breath mints are great for our mouth. Why don't we have shoe mints for when the tongue of our shoe has bad breath?

By the word of the Lord the heavens were made, and by the breath of his mouth all their host.

Psalm 33:6

#273

White Out is a liquid or tape used to correct mistakes on white paper. Do you think it's discriminatory that we don't have the same thing for colored paper?

My brothers, show no partiality as you hold the faith in our Lord Jesus Christ, the Lord of glory.

James 2:1

#274

What is the definition of *cloud storage*? Cloud storage is the place on cloud nine where you store all your elevated thoughts and lofty ideas for access on a rainy day.

Like clouds and wind without rain is a man who boasts of a gift he does not give.

Proverbs 25:14

#275

If the assignment is to "live the dream," will nightmares be accepted in fulfillment of this requirement?

"And in the last days it shall be, God declares, that I will pour out my Spirit on all flesh, and your sons and your daughters shall prophesy, and your young men shall see visions, and your old men shall dream dreams."

Acts 2:17

#276

We need so many human touches a day to be emotionally healthy. We touch our phones hundreds or thousands of times a day. Shouldn't that make our phones feel extremely loved?

"Let the children come to me; do not hinder them, for to such belongs the kingdom of God. Truly, I say to you, whoever does not receive the kingdom of God like a child shall not enter it." And he took them in his arms and blessed them, laying his hands on them.

Mark 10:14b- 16

#277

Did you know I'm a frequent flyer? I take one flight after the next at work every day. It's because I prefer stairs to elevators.

"If you make me an altar of stone, you shall not build it of hewn stones, for if you wield your tool on it you profane it. And you shall not go up by steps to my altar, that your nakedness be not exposed on it."

Exodus 20:25- 26

#278

Have you ever attended a ribbon cutting ceremony? If so, then you know first-hand it announces the grand opening of a building by the ceremonial cutting of a ribbon strung across its entrance. When I opened my own business, I saved time and cut right through the lengthy ceremony by buying a pre-cut ribbon.

Then the king and all the people offered sacrifice before the LORD. King Solomon offered as a sacrifice 22,000 oxen and 120,000 sheep. So the king and all the people dedicated the house of God.

2 Chronicles 7:4, 5

#279

When measuring time, distance, or quantity, we usually estimate and respond in multiples of five. We say things like, "I'll be ready in five minutes." Why do we speak in fives? I think it's because we have five digits on each hand. That's a handy thing to know. I'm glad I could put my finger on the answer.

My son, keep my words and treasure up my commandments with you; keep my commandments and live; keep my teaching as the apple of your eye; bind them on your fingers; write them on the tablet of your heart.

Proverbs 7:1- 3

#280

Do you know the catch phrase of all cool puppets? Hang loose!

"You did not choose me, but I chose you and appointed you that you should go and bear fruit and that your fruit should abide, so that whatever you ask the Father in my name, he may give it to you."

John 15:16

#281

Is the *International Date Line* a line you stand in to date internationals?

"When a stranger sojourns with you in your land, you shall not do him wrong. You shall treat the stranger who sojourns with you as the native among you, and you shall love him as yourself, for you were strangers in the land of Egypt: I am the Lord your God."

Leviticus 19:33- 34

#282

At some coffee shops and restaurants, they ask for your name so they can call it when your order is ready. What do people with amnesia do in these situations?

"I have an order ready for X!"

"For I will be merciful toward their iniquities, and I will remember their sins no more."

Hebrews 8:12

#283

Most people don't like to wait in line, but what about a weight in line buffet? This is a new buffet where they weigh the customers before and after they eat. Then, they charge them a set amount for each ounce they gain. This type of food service system gives a whole new meaning to watching your weight, doesn't it?

The next day Moses sat to judge the people, and the people stood around Moses from morning till evening.

Exodus 18:13

#284

Isn't it better to hear, "I'll take care of you over here," from a cashier than from a mobster?

Take care, brothers, lest there be in any of you an evil, unbelieving heart, leading you to fall away from the living God.

Hebrews 3:12

#285

Some people say, "The journey is just as important as the destination." I don't think crash test dummies say this about either the journey or the destination. Yes, of course I know crash test dummies can't talk. What kind of dummy do you think I am?

But I do not account my life of any value nor as precious to myself, if only I may finish my course and the ministry that I received from the Lord Jesus, to testify to the gospel of the grace of God.

Acts 20:24

#286

Shouldn't Monday be in the middle of the week? That way we would be able to get a few work days under our belt before we must deal with Monday.

And on the seventh day God finished his work that he had done, and he rested on the seventh day from all his work that he had done. So God blessed the seventh day and made it holy, because on it God rested from all his work that he had done in creation.

Genesis 2:2- 3

#287

We have scarecrows to keep crows away from corn fields. Why don't we have a similar thing to keep insects away from our gardens? We could call them scarebugs.

Then from the smoke came locusts on the earth, and they were given power like the power of scorpions of the earth. They were told not to harm the grass of the earth or any green plant or any tree, but only those people who do not have the seal of God on their foreheads.

Revelation 9:3, 4

#288

What is a conundrum? I know conundrum is not a percussion instrument, but it beats the heck out of me how to play it.

Praise him with sounding cymbals; praise him with loud clashing cymbals! Let everything that has breath praise the Lord! Praise the Lord!

Psalm 150:5- 6

A Look into Psalm 100

Shout, serve, and sing to the LORD with joy,
Come before Him and these things employ.

The LORD is God, this we'll discuss,
We are not our creators, but God made us.

We are His people, the work of His hand,
The sheep of His pasture follow him in a band.

Enter His gates with a thankful heart,
Come into His courts with all praise and not part.

A great man this point did raise,
When speaking on the subject of praise:

"Praise is not just the expression of joy,
Praise truly is the completion of joy."1

So, give to the Giver abundant gratitude,
And bless the Blesser with praise in this attitude.

Why should we do all these things you do ask?
It seems like a lot, perhaps a burdening task.

For the LORD is good, and gives what is right,
We should worship His name both day and night.

God is eternal and so is His love,
In goodness he pours it out from above.

His provision is faithful, it's never late,
Another like Him you will never locate.

So, to the Greatest, let us the greatest things bring,
Shout, serve, and sing with joy to our king.

1 Lewis, C. S., Reflections on the Psalms. New York: A Harvest Book/ Harcourt, Inc., 1986

#289

Did you know that headphones are useless for making long-distance calls? It's like you're on continual hold with background music playing.

There Zadok the priest took the horn of oil from the tent and anointed Solomon. Then they blew the trumpet, and all the people said, "Long live King Solomon!" And all the people went up after him, playing on pipes, and rejoicing with great joy, so that the earth was split by their noise.

1 Kings 1:39- 40

#290

Did you hear about the anti-tax lobbyist who proposed a bill for the reduction of the month of April to only fourteen days, while increasing the month of March to forty-seven days?

Pay to all what is owed to them: taxes to whom taxes are owed, revenue to whom revenue is owed, respect to whom respect is owed, honor to whom honor is owed.

Romans 13:7

#291

Since we seem to find things in the last place we look for them, why don't people look for lost things in the last place, first? Looks like I just shortened your search by finding the ideal solution regarding missing things.

"Or what woman, having ten silver coins, if she loses one coin, does not light a lamp and sweep the house and seek diligently until she finds it? And when she has found it, she calls together her friends and neighbors, saying, 'Rejoice with me for I have found the coin that I had lost.' Just so, I tell you, there is joy before the angels of God over one sinner who repents."

Luke 15:8- 10

#292

What would a valley girl librarian say?

"Like, gag me with the total flatware book section!"

Even though I walk through the valley of the shadow of death, I will fear no evil, for you are with me; your rod and your staff, they comfort me.

Psalm 23:4

#293

If sports teams used massage chairs instead of benches, then it would be easier for a player to accept when he or she is benched.

"Coach, are you massage chairing me again? Great!"

Your throne, O God, is forever and ever. The scepter of your kingdom is a scepter of uprightness

Psalm 45:6

#294

I'm thinking about starting a rock band. What do you think of the name *Police Cars* for our band? I've already written a lot of great songs, such as *Black Coffee and White Donuts, Step Away from the Car, Hand's in the Air, License and Registration Please, and Have a Good Day and Drive Safe.*

"For you shall go out in joy and be led forth in peace; the mountains and the hills before you shall break forth into singing, and all the trees of the field shall clap their hands."

Isaiah 55:12

#295

Why is it that when someone says, "This place is a real zoo!" they are rarely at a zoo when they say it?

Now out of the ground the Lord God had formed every beast of the field and every bird of the heavens and brought them to the man to see what he would call them. And whatever the man called every living creature, that was its name.

Genesis 2:19

Organ Mountains
Las Cruces, NM

Beautiful music fills my ears and heart
But others may only hear the wind
Sweeping between the granite mountain pillars

#296

Do people that are certifiably insane receive a certificate for that?

And David rose and fled that day from Saul and went to Achish the king of Gath. And the servants of Achish said to him, "Is not this David the king of the land? Did they not sing to one another of him in dances, 'Saul has struck down his thousands, and David his ten thousands'?"
And David took these words to heart and was much afraid of Achish the king of Gath. So he changed his behavior before them and pretended to be insane in their hands and made marks on the doors of the gate and let his spittle run down his beard.

1 Samuel 21:10- 13

#297

Can you define abandoned?

abandoned: v. when a musician misses the band bus and is left behind

And they abandoned the Lord, the God of their fathers, who had brought them out of the land of Egypt. They went after other gods, from among the gods of the peoples who were around them, and bowed down to them. And they provoked the Lord to anger.

Judges 2:12

#298

Why do people love material things so much? When you love your possessions, they won't love you back. It's a one-sided affair.

Do not love the world or the things in the world. If anyone loves the world, the love of the Father is not in him. For all that is in the world—the desires of the flesh and the desires of the eyes and pride of life—is not from the Father but is from the world.

1 John 2:15- 16

#299

Cities install speed breakers on streets as obstacles of progress, to slow the traffic down to a safe speed. Depending on where you live, these ridges in the road are called speed bumps, speed humps, a traffic calming measure, silent policeman, or sleeping policeman. If we really wanted to install obstacles of progress for drivers, then why don't we put ditches across the road? We could call them open policeman graves.

"For as the Father has life in himself, so he has granted the Son also to have life in himself. And he has given him authority to execute judgment, because he is the Son of Man. Do not marvel at this, for an hour is coming when all who are in the tombs will hear his voice and come out, those who have done good to the resurrection of life, and those who have done evil to the resurrection of judgment."

John 5:26- 29

#300

What do you think of my new rapper name, $2.99?

Yo, doesn't it make mo' cents than the rapper name 50 Cent?

Do you hear what I'm sayin'?

My new rap name is money in the bank plus interest

My rhyme account's in shape, financial strength, got fitness,

If you don't know that you're livin' in the red

Overdrawn, your credit score is dead

Insufficient funds, you're in over your head

Check this, check your bank statement

My gold bank card is full of rhymes

Depositing lyrics, just in time

Available to you, all the time

Wire transfer on the go

Fill it up yo

$2.99 in the house!

A good name is to be chosen rather than great riches, and favor is better than silver or gold.

Proverbs 22:1

Extra Questions to Ponder

#1

Why do people ask me if they can pay me a visit? I tell them no, you can visit me for free.

#2

Do you like to go horseback riding and bird-watching at the same time? If your answer is yes, then, take your birdwatching to new heights. Ride a Pegasus.

#3

Why is lobbyist a profession? I never understood why people are paid to stand in a lobby.

#4

Have you heard the saying, "You have to meet people where they're at"?
I agree, because you cannot meet people where they are not at.

#5

Why did the inventers of badminton give a bad name to a good sport? Why couldn't it have been named goodminton?

#6

Are you a person who sees the glass as half-full, or half-empty? Why not stop focusing on the level, and just be grateful you have a glass?

#7

Is a chimenea a stove for cooking chimichangas?

#8

Why are "mind blowing" experiences seen as a good thing? I would like my brain to remain intact.

#9

People build castles in the sand. Why aren't people more realistic with their beach home sculptures? If they were, we might see more sand apartments.

#10

If the lion is the king of the jungle, then why isn't the sea lion the king of the sea?

#11

If the store is difficult to get to because of road construction, can it still be called a convenience store?

#12

Is it true that everyone loves? Yes, some love to hate, while others love to love.

#13

What kind of tie should you wear to an archery banquet? A bow tie.

#14

How are an almost-full cemetery and an author with writer's block similar? They are both running out of plots.

#15

Did you hear about my new beverage coaster I invented? It's a drink coaster with wheels so that you can move it about without leaving a trail of water. It's called a roller coaster.

#16

Do you enjoy visiting new places? I was visiting a place for the first time and one of the residents asked me, "Are you new?"
I said, "No, I'm fifty-three years old."

#17

Did you hear about the environmentally-conscious electric eel? He converted to solar power.

#18

When people ask me, "Why are you here?"
I reply, "Isn't it obvious? I'm here because I'm not somewhere else."

#19

Do people have trouble appreciating your genius? Occasionally people do say to me, "You just spoke a pearl of wisdom!" Mostly, though, they just tell me to clam up.

#20

Why don't people have birthday parties in the hospital when their children are born? It's the day of their birth.

#21

Did you know that clocks get upset when people are late? Yes—it really ticks them off.

#22

Why aren't oceans known for their friendliness? They do wave a lot at people.

#23

Did you know there are some things money can't buy? Like bankruptcy.

#24

Since airplanes have life vests under the seats, shouldn't passenger ships have parachutes under the seats?

#25

If a safe is broken into and all the valuables are robbed, should it then be called an unsafe?

#26

If handguns were banned, what would they use at track meets to signal the start of the race?

#27

Is it okay to wear sandals where there is no sand?

#28

Do you love diversity? I love diversity because it adds so much to our experience. People come in different colors: yellow, brown, white, black—and that's just their teeth.

#29

What is something you should never say during your driver's license eye test?
"What eye chart?"

#30

Would you like to be a comedian? I know I'm funny, because a lot of people say my life's a joke.

#31

Did you know there's a place for a fire? It's called a fireplace.

#32

Do you take fish oil pills? I've been taking fish oil pills for three months, but I can't tell that I swim any better now than before.

#33

Have you ever received unusual instructions concerning a party you were invited to?

It beats the heck out of me why my friends want me to come to their son's birthday party dressed up as a piñata.

#34

Did you know that musicians who play elevator music don't make a lot of money?
Elevators just can't hold very large crowds for live performances.

#35

Are highway interchanges shaped like four-leaf clovers to make drivers luckier?

Shadow Casters

At three o'clock in the afternoon, on Second Avenue, I walked under the hot summer sky. I pulled myself along the sidewalk through the thick humid air. My shadow, cast on the gray-walled building alongside me, made me look slightly rounder than I imagine myself to be. For a brief moment I was discouraged, feeling my diet had been in vain. But distortion is the game of shadows.

Coming to the corner of the edifice, my shadow folded, with one half on the east side, and the other on the south side. For a moment I possessed the ability of a contortionist.

Turning the corner, my shadow regained its normal shape except that it stretched a little bit longer than before. Walking on the wall like a black spider man, my shadow defied gravity without the least fanfare. This was just his usual afternoon stroll. Matching step for step, my detail-less shadow accompanied me without one complaint of the heat.

I bought a cup of coffee. Standing inside the shop near the window, I saw my faintly-cast shadow also held a cup in his hand; it was a two for the price of one special. My shadow and I walked outside and sat on a wooden bench facing the street. My body sat squarely on the deep bench, while my shadow sat half on the seat, and half on the grass before us.

We both watched the people as they passed by. Their shadows were tilted and kept pace by their sides like heeling dogs. Occasionally, a stranger's shadow would touch mine as they walked past. All people need a certain amount of human touches every day. I wonder if shadows feel the same way.

I saw someone I knew on the opposite side of the street. I waved. Following my lead, my shadow waved at his shadow, except my shadow's wave swept across the sidewalk and into the street. My shadow and I watched as my friend walked eastward. Halfway up the street his shadow took the lead and walked in front of him like a guide on a city tour.

I sipped my coffee and so did my shadow. Our thirsts are synchronized. I never have coffee alone while the sun shines. I'm sure my shadow likes his coffee black. We both have so much in common.

Looking up I saw another friend of mine approaching on our side of the street. "Hello," I said.

"How are you?"

"I'm fine," she replied.

I glanced down to see our shadows standing lip to lip. Immediately I pulled my head back, so as not to appear fresh with her. She stood and talked at length with me. She is so beautiful. One day I will ask her out on a date. I looked down again, and our shadows had moved with the passing of time. Once more they were lip to lip. I took a half-step back, causing a separation between them. I wish I was as confident with women as my shadow is.

We waved goodbye to each other. She walked away, leaving my shadow and I to finish our coffee. I was still on the bench, but my shadow now sat fully in the grass. In his nice black clothing too! Upon further observation I noticed that my shadow was twice my height. I admit I took a moment to enjoy this affiliation, since I am short in stature. I decided I could overlook his undignified position on the grass.

A loud sound echoed off the buildings all around me, snapping my attention back out of the shadow land. A driver was dashing out of his car to examine the pedestrian who lay in front of it. My shadow and I ran over to see the condition of the man. He and his shadow were both unconscious on the ground. The man lay with red blood spots scattered around him, and his shadow with black blood spots alongside.

Within moments, it seemed, an ambulance came and took the man to the hospital. I managed to learn the man's name was Cliff. I looked back to where he had lain. It was empty except for the red and black spots. His shadow was gone. They must have put him into the ambulance when I was not looking.

I cried for the man's misfortune and said a prayer for him that he would recover. With my head still slightly bowed, I looked at my shadow. I could not tell if he too was shedding tears.

The next day I read the obituaries. My shadow looked over my shoulder. I saw Cliff's name, and though I did not know him, I decided to attend to his funeral. It seemed right, since we had spent a brief moment together before he passed.

Beside Cliff's grave I listened intently to the preacher as he stood at the head of the casket.

"'O LORD,'" the preacher quoted, "'what is man that you regard him, or the son of man that you think of him? Man is like a breath; his days are like a passing shadow.' These are the words of King David from Psalm chapter one hundred forty-four, verses three and four. Our lives are brief. We must live them serving others. Our shadows should fall on the orphans, widows, poor, strangers and others as we meet their needs. We must actively live our lives to glorify God and enjoy him forever. This must be our goal in this short life. For in this way dwells true life. We must press on until our body is laid below the earth, hid from the light, never to cast a shadow again. We are shadow casters here in the land of the living. Though Cliff is gone, his life and shadow has touched our lives. Cliff trusted in Jesus Christ. All those who are in Christ will one day reunite with Cliff, and with the Lord in the land where no shadows exist. Let us pray."

My shadow and I both bowed our heads.

The River

The Oklahoma countryside in springtime can be like a patch of heaven. On this warm afternoon, honeysuckle permeated the air with its sweet aroma. Dragonflies hovered at the water's edge. Bees dropped in to extract their precious cargo from the honeysuckle and neighboring trumpet flowers. Vigorously, cardinals and scissortails crisscrossed the grass as they gathered food for their young. A few puffy clouds floated lazily overhead. Butterflies played tag with one another.

Despite this display, William walked the trail with his head down, kicking rocks as he went. He was blind to the beauty around him as he descended toward the river bank. What was he going to do with his life? All his friends had secured good jobs and were making a living. His most recent rejection at an interview was still stinging him. William's discouragement hung on him like a metal suit. He needed to get away to think. He pressed on toward the river bottom. William felt his thoughts might be less noisy alongside the ripple of the river. It was the perfect place to sit, meditate and not be bothered.

"What is it I should do?"

The question kept running through his mind. His future seemed to be like a door that he could not open, no matter how hard he tried.

As he arrived at the river he walked to its edge and gazed into the slow-moving water. His reflection stared back at him with a troubled look. He picked up a rock and tossed it in, temporarily removing his problematic reflection. The clear blue water steadily moved downstream. In a few seconds his reflection came back to haunt him. He thought, "My life is slowly going downstream like this river, and what do I have to show for it?"

He withdrew to the bank and sat down. The whole area was active and busy. All of nature around him had a job, a focus and a purpose. They did not doubt what they were supposed to do with their lives. Why was it so difficult for him? Where did they get their direction? He leaned back and looked up into the sky watching the clouds drift.

"It's not fair. I want to know what I should do with my life. I don't want to sit idly by while everyone else lives their life. I don't want to be left behind floundering in my own despair."

He lowered his head as he sunk into deeper discouragement. He thought of prayer, but he did not feel like praying. He forced a quick petition asking God to give him direction, and held his eyes closed for a while after he prayed, thinking of where he might look for a job. Opening them, he looked around. The river community seemed to be speaking to him. William reached into his front shirt pocket and pulled out a pen and a small notebook that he was using to keep track of the jobs he had applied for.

He scribbled down thoughts as they rushed into his head. William loved to write. He had written some pretty good stories and poetry in the past, but now the lines seemed to flow like the river—steady and consistent. It was as if his writing flowered, emitting a powerfully fragrant story. The dark clouds rolled back from his thoughts, and as he wrote, a small smile appeared on his face. He held his pen still and then said, "Is this what I was looking for?" He felt calm within.

"Am I supposed to be a writer?" This time the prayer wasn't forced. "God, you do answer prayer. If

I had only prayed sooner instead of trying to solve my problems on my own, I could have saved myself a lot of grief. Is this your way of telling me to write? I'm listening!"

William wrote until the sun was almost set. He walked back to his house with purpose in his step, and a renewed confidence in prayer, ready to see where his writing journey might take him.

Poetry Index

Poetry Index

A Look into Psalm 100	172 - 173
Canine Conditions	67
Cloud Crown	7
Creative Words	39
End of the Cruise	100 - 101
Few	161
Future Visit	123
Ground Coffee	83
Living Memories	113
One Last Stroke	26
Onomatopoeia	15
Organ Mountains	178
Raining Tears	88
Rescued	131
Resurrection	138
Revelation 3:20	49 - 50
Scheduled Quake	55
Supportive	92

Rodney Charles Dutton grew up in southern Oklahoma. He has lived in every time zone of the lower forty-eight states of the U.S.A. He has also visited twenty-six countries and had the privilege of living in India for three years. Rodney loves learning about history, cultures and languages. Diversity intrigues him, and he feels comfortable in multicultural settings. Photography fascinates him. Creating and sharing his short stories, children's stories and poetry give him great joy. Rodney currently lives in New York City. You can contact the author at RodneyCharlesDutton@yahoo.com

Books by Rodney Charles Dutton

Available on Amazon and Kindle

For Adults:

Above, Beside, Below: Poetry by Rodney Charles Dutton

Unusual Sayings for Usual Days: Readings for
Amusement and Action

For Children:

Candice Goes to The City

Cason Goes to the Dentist

Lisa's Fabric World

Look At That! The Life of Francine the Watchful Cat
(Children's Storybook)

Look At That! The Life of Francine the Watchful Cat
(Children's Companion Activity Book)

Please Don't Cry: The Story of the Compassionate Onion

Sammy and the Soda Fountain

Walk Toward Your Dream: The Tale of Jake the Snake

Made in the USA
Monee, IL
13 June 2020

32607316R00115